Latin Synonyms for Language Lovers

A Select Thesaurus

By

Christine E. Meyer

Bolchazy-Carducci Publishers, Inc.

Mundelein, Illinois USA

Editor: Bridget Dean
Contributing Editor: Laurel Draper
Design & Layout: Adam Phillip Velez
Illustrations: Lydia Koller
Cover Image: Clio, muse of history, holding writing tablets. Detail from the "Muses Sarcophagus," representing the nine Muses and their attributes. Marble, first half of the 2nd century CE, found by the Via Ostiense. Musée du Louvre.

Latin Synonyms for Language Lovers
A Select Thesaurus

Christine E. Meyer

© 2013 Bolchazy-Carducci Publishers, Inc.

Bolchazy-Carducci Publishers, Inc.
1570 Baskin Road
Mundelein, Illinois 60060
www.bolchazy.com

Printed in the United States of America
2013
by United Graphics

ISBN 978-0-86516-794-0

Library of Congress Cataloging-in-Publication Data

Meyer, Christine E. (Classicist)
  Latin synonyms for language lovers : a select thesaurus / by Christine E. Meyer.
    pages cm
  Includes bibliographical references and index.
  ISBN 978-0-86516-794-0 (pbk. : alk. paper) 1. Latin language--Synonyms and antonyms.
I. Title.
  PA2349.M49 2013
  473'.12--dc23

                                                                        2013017829

Ōlim prōgenitor Calaber servābat onustās
Arcās scrībendī. Neptis scrīptor sum.
Nostrōs discipulōs hortēmur ut sīc aliōrsum
Linguās antīquās expōnant vīvē.

• Table of Contents

• List of Illustrations

• Acknowledgements

The notion for this book came to me after I spent a week writing Latin poetry with other Latin-language enthusiasts. Sponsored by the University of Michigan classics department, the creative week made us all realize the necessity of finding synonyms in order to meet the demands of meter. Thus, I owe the genesis of this work to Gina Soter and David Money, the *prīncipēs* of our week.

A further impetus for this book came in teaching Latin to my students at Downingtown West High School. As a way to assist the students in remembering and recognizing vocabulary, I suggested they create "synonym maps," or diagrams with illustrations of like-meaning words. Thus, I defer to my students in their willingness to incorporate a new practice and to stay the course over the years.

One student in particular, Faith Bull, took it upon herself to assist in the research for this thesaurus. Faith's consistency, encouragement, and joy catapulted this opus into its ultimate being.

Finally, I thank Bolchazy-Carducci Publishers for recognizing the value of a thesaurus. Allan, Bridget, et al. have facilitated once again the Latin fluency of generations.

• How to Use This Book

This book is designed to appeal broadly to users of Latin, from students, to teachers, to armchair Latinists. It facilitates the reading, writing, and speaking of Latin. In addition, it should appeal to anyone who wants to expand his or her cache of English vocabulary.

The purposes of providing the meanings of words in categories are several. First, words are grouped together so as to allow them to be understood conjointly, under one umbrella. Because students often confuse certain vocabulary words, the placement of such words with others of like meanings helps with clarification. The words provided in each category belong to the particular vocabularies of Caesar, Vergil, Horace, Ovid, and others. Thus, when the student grasps the meanings of the words in a group, he has immediate access to the vocabulary that appears in the major authors.

A second purpose of the thesaurus is to provide a ready resource for the learning of grammatical forms. Words are organized according to part of speech. Then, the words in each category are listed according to declension (if nouns) or conjugation (if verbs). Thus, the teacher or student can isolate one form from the others as a basis for particular practice.

Third, teachers and students can benefit from having synonyms with which to interact in conversation or in paraphrasing texts. In addition, writers of Latin will have multiple options for composition, and writers of poetry, specifically, will benefit. Since meter depends on syllables and sound, often finding a synonym or an alternate expression will solve a poet's metrical problem.

Finally, because Latin provides the basis for nearly two-thirds of the English language, exposure to the lists of synonyms will enhance one's ability to recognize the roots of English words and to anticipate the meanings of unknown words.

• VERBS

• AFFLICTING, INJURING, WOUNDING

Regular

1st Conjugation

afflīctō, afflīctāre, afflīctāvī, afflīctātus	distress, torment, injure, ruin
cōnflīctō, cōnflīctāre, cōnflīctāvī, cōnflīctātus	ruin
excruciō, excruciāre, excruciāvī, excruciātus	torment, afflict, harass
foedō, foedāre, foedāvī, foedātus	wound, mutilate, defile
laniō, laniāre, laniāvī, laniātus	tear, shred, mutilate, lacerate
mactō, mactāre, mactāvī, mactātus	afflict, punish, overthrow
violō, violāre, violāvī, violātus	to treat with violence, injure, dishonor, violate
vulnerō, vulnerāre, vulnerāvī, vulnerātus	to wound, hurt, injure, maim

2nd Conjugation

noceō, nocēre, nocuī, nocitum (+ dat)	hurt, harm, injure

3rd Conjugation

adflīgō, adflīgere, adflīxī, adflīctus	damage, hurt, injure, distress
angō, angere	vex, torment, trouble
corrumpō, corrumpere, corrūpī, corruptus	destroy, ruin, injure, spoil
laedō, laedere, laesī, laesus	hurt, wound, damage, injure, afflict
prōscindō, prōscindere, prōscidī, prōscissus	satirize, revile, defame

3rd io Conjugation

adficiō, adficere, adfēcī, adfectus	afflict, weaken, oppress, impair

Irregular

obsum, obesse, obfuī (+ dat)	hurt, injure, be harmful to

• Approaching

Regular

1st Conjugation

adventō, adventāre, adventāvī, adventātum	approach, march on, advance
appropinquō, appropinquāre, appropinquāvī (+ dat)	approach, draw near, come near
propinquō, propinquāre, propinquāvī, propinquātum (+ dat)	approach, draw near

2nd Conjugation

admoveō, admovēre, admōvī, admōtus	approach, move to, move towards

3rd Conjugation

accēdō, accēdere, accessī, accessum	go to, come to, approach, come near
incēdō, incēdere, incessī, incessum	approach, advance, march, arrive
succēdō, succēdere, successī, successus	approach, march to, draw near

Deponent

3rd io Conjugation

aggredior, aggredī, aggressus sum	approach

Irregular

adeō, adīre, adiī/adīvī, aditus	come to, approach, draw near

• ARRIVING

Regular

3rd Conjugation

attingō, attingere, attigī, attāctus	reach, arrive at, arrive near, border

4th Conjugation

adveniō, advenīre, advēnī, adventum	arrive, come to, reach
dēveniō, dēvenīre, dēvēnī, dēventum	come, arrive, reach
perveniō, pervenīre, pervēnī, perventus	reach, come up, arrive, attain

Deponent

3rd Conjugation

adipīscor, adipīscī, adeptus sum	arrive at, reach to
appellor, appellī, appulsus sum	land, put in at

• ASKING

Regular

1st Conjugation

flāgitō, flāgitāre, flāgitāvī, flāgitātus	demand urgently, require, entreat
interrogō, interrogāre, interrogāvī, interrogātus	ask, inquire, question, interrogate
invītō, invītāre, invītāvī, invītātus	ask, request, invite, entertain, treat, feast
postulō, postulāre, postulāvī, postulātus	ask, demand, request, desire, call for
rogitō, rogitāre, rogitāvī, rogitātus	keep asking, ask eagerly
rogō, rogāre, rogāvī, rogātus	ask, request, question, interrogate
sententiam rogō (+ acc)	ask the opinion of, call upon to vote

3rd Conjugation

cōnsulō, cōnsulere, cōnsuluī, cōnsultus (+ dat)	consult, deliberate, take thought for, consider the interests of, ask for advice, ask one's opinion
dēposcō, dēposcere, dēpoposcī	demand, request, claim
exposcō, exposcere, expoposcī	demand, ask earnestly, beg, request
pōscō, pōscere, popōscī	ask urgently, beg, demand, request, desire
quaerō, quaerere, quaesīvī, quaesītus	ask, desire, require, demand, need, call for
repōscō, repōscere	demand back, ask again, require, ask for
requīrō, requīrere, requīsīvī, requīsītus	ask, inquire for, demand, seek to know

Deponent

1st Conjugation

percontor, percontārī, percontātus sum	ask particularly, inquire, interrogate
scītor, scītārī, scītātus sum	ask, inquire, seek to know

• Being Present

Regular

1st Conjugation

exstō, exstāre, exstitī	be conspicuous, stand out
īnstō, īnstāre, īnstitī	be at hand, impend, take a position

3rd Conjugation

suppetō, suppetere, suppetiī/suppetīvī, suppetītum	be at hand, be available, be present

Deponent

1st Conjugation

versor, versārī, versātus sum	be present, be engaged, be situated

Irregular

adsum, adesse, adfuī, adfutūrus	be present, be at hand, be at, give attention
intersum, interesse, interfuī	attend, be present, take part

• Bearing, Bringing

Regular

1st Conjugation

aggregō, aggregāre, aggregāvī, aggregātus	bring together in a flock, collect
apportō, apportāre, apportāvī, apportātus	bring along, carry, convey
dēportō, dēportāre, dēportāvī, dēportātus	carry away, bring home, take along
portō, portāre, portāvī, portātus	bear, convey, carry, take, bring
supportō, supportāre, supportāvī, supportātus	bring up, convey

3rd Conjugation

advehō, advehere, advexī, advectus	carry to, bring to
āvehō, āvehere, āvexī, āvectus	carry off, take away
committō, committere, commīsī, commissus	bring together, bring together in a fight, abandon (a child)
dēmō, dēmere, dēmpsī, dēmptus	take away, remove, withdraw
dēprōmō, dēprōmere, dēprōmpsī, dēprōmptus	draw out, bring out, fetch
gerō, gerere, gessī, gestus	bear, carry, wear, bring
gīgnō, gīgnere, genuī, genitus	bear, bring forth, give birth to
pervehō, pervehere, pervexī, pervectus	bear through, convey through, carry, bring

Irregular

adferō, adferre, attulī, adlātus	bring, fetch, carry in, convey
cōnferō, cōnferre, contulī, conlātus	bring together, collect, bring, bring together in thought
dēferō, dēferre, dētulī, dēlatus	bring away, carry off, deliver
ferō, ferre, tulī, lātus	bear, carry, take
īnferō, īnferre, intulī, illātus	bring in, bring to, carry in, introduce, bring for burial

• Begging

Regular

1st Conjugation

implōrō, implōrāre, implōrāvī, implōrātus	call for aid, entreat, beg, beseech, implore
obsecrō, obsecrāre, obsecrāvī, obsecrātus	entreat, beseech, implore, supplicate
ōrō, ōrāre, ōrāvī, ōrātus	pray, beg, entreat, beseech, implore

3rd Conjugation

quaesō, quaesere	beg, pray, entreat, beseech (only in first person sing and pl, present)

Deponent

1st Conjugation

dēprecor, dēprecārī, dēprecātus sum	avert by prayer, plead against, beg to escape, pray for, plead with
obtestor, obtestārī, obtestātus sum	entreat, beseech, supplicate, call as a witness, conjure
precor, precārī, precātus sum	beg, call upon, beseech, entreat

• BEGINNING

Regular

1st Conjugation

coeptō, coeptāre, coeptāvī, coeptātus	begin, begin eagerly, undertake
incohō (inchoō), incohāre, incohāvī, incohātus	begin, start, begin to discuss, propose
initiō, initiāre, initiāvī, initiātus	begin, initiate, consecrate
occeptō, occeptāre, occeptāvī, occeptātus	begin

3rd Conjugation

capessō, capessere, capessiī/capessīvī, capessītus	take in hand, undertake, enter upon
committō, committere, commīsī, commissus	begin, engage in, fight
īnstituō, īnstituere, īnstituī, īnstitūtus	begin, commence, undertake, found
integrāscō, integrāscere	begin anew, break out afresh

3rd io Conjugation

concipiō, concipere, concēpī, conceptus	conceive, become pregnant
incipiō, incipere, incēpī, inceptus	begin, take in hand, originate

Deponent

4th Conjugation

ōrdior, ōrdīrī, ōrsus sum	begin, commence, set about, undertake

Irregular/Defective

coepī, coepisse, coeptus	to have begun (only in pft and plupft)
coepiō, coepī, coeptus	begin, commence
concieō, conciēre, concīvī, concītus	instigate, rouse, excite, stir up, provoke, inspire
ineo, inīre, iniī/inīvī, initus	begin a journey, enter upon, begin, undertake

• Building

Regular

1st Conjugation

aedificō, aedificāre, aedificāvī, aedificātus	build, erect a building, construct, erect
contabulō, contabulāre, contabulāvī, contabulātus	floor over, build in stories
exaedificō, exaedificāre, exaedificāvī, exaedificātus	build, construct, finish building

3rd Conjugation

compōnō, compōnere, composuī, compositus	construct, build, compose, write
condō, condere, condidī, conditus	found, build, erect, be the author of
dūcō, dūcere, dūxī, ductus	erect, construct, shape
exstruō, exstruere, exstrūxī, exstrūctus	build up, construct, fill with buildings, build in imagination
īnstituō, īnstituere, īnstituī, īnstitūtus	set up, found, establish, build, fabricate
īnstruō, īnstruere, īnstruxī, īnstructus	build in, insert, form, set in order, equip
perdūcō, perdūcere, perdūxī, perductus aquam	build an aqueduct
struō, struere, struxī, structus	build, erect, fabricate, construct

3rd io Conjugation

iaciō, iacere, iēcī, iactus	establish, build, found, construct
perficiō, perficere, perfēcī, perfectus	build, accomplish, finish, complete

Deponent

4th Conjugation

mōlior, mōlīrī, mōlītus sum	build, make, erect, construct

• BURNING

Regular

1st Conjugation

cōnflagrō, cōnflagrāre, cōnflagrāvī, cōnflagrātus	burn, be on fire, be consumed
cremō, cremāre, cremāvī, cremātus	burn, consume by fire
dēflagrō, dēflagrāre, dēflagrāvī, dēflagrātus	burn out, burn down, consume with fire
flagrō, flagrāre, flagrāvī	burn, flame, blaze, glow
flammō, flammāre, flammāvī, flammātus	kindle, blaze, burn, inflame
īnflammō, īnflammāre, īnflammāvī, īnflammātus	set on fire, kindle, inflame, excite
ustulō, ustulāre, ustulāvī, ustulātus	consume by fire, burn up

2nd Conjugation

ārdeō, ārdēre, ārsī, ārsūrus	burn, be on fire, be in turmoil, blaze
ferveō, fervēre	seethe, burn
torreō, torrēre, torruī, tostus	burn, scorch

3rd Conjugation

accendō, accendere, accendī, accensus	set on fire, stir up
combūrō, combūrere, combūssī, combūstus	burn up
exārdēscō, exārdēscere, exārsī, exārsum	burst into flames
exūrō, exūrere, exūssī, exūstus	burn up
incendō, incendere, incendī, incensus	inflame
inūrō, inūrere, inūssī, inūstus (+ dat)	burn into, brand into
praeūrō, praeūrere, praeūssī, praeūstus	burn in front, burn at the end
succendō, succendere, succendī, succensus	set on fire
urō, urere, ūssī, ūstus	burn, inflame

3rd io Conjugation

incendiō, incendere, incensī, incensus	burn

• CHOOSING

Regular	
1st Conjugation	
creō, creāre, creāvī, creātus	produce, create, elect, choose
dēsignō, dēsignāre, dēsignāvī, dēsignātus	point out, appoint, choose, elect
optō, optāre, optāvī, optātus	choose, select
praeoptō, praeoptāre, praeoptāvī, praeoptātus	prefer
2nd Conjugation	
faveō, favēre, fāvī, fautum (+ dat)	favor
3rd Conjugation	
dēligō, dēligere, dēlēgī, delēctus	choose
ēligō, ēligere, ēlēgī, ēlēctus	select
excerpō, excerpere, excerpsī, excerptus	select
legō, legere, lēgī, lēctus	gather, choose, read

Deponent	
4th Conjugation	
sortior, sortīrī, sortītus sum	select, choose

Irregular	
malō, mālle, māluī (+ infin)	choose, rather, prefer

• Climbing

Regular

3rd Conjugation

ascendō, ascendere, ascendī, ascensus	climb, mount, go up
cōnscendō, cōnscendere, cōnscendī, cōnscēnsus	mount (a horse), climb, go on board
ēscendō, ēscendere, ēscendī, ēscensus	climb up, mount, ascend
scandō, scandere, scandī, scānsus	climb, ascend, mount, rise
trānscendō, trānscendere, trānscendī, trānscensus	climb over, cross over, surmount

• CONCEALING, COVERING

Regular

1st Conjugation

cēlō, cēlāre, cēlāvī, cēlātus	hide
dissimulō, dissimulāre, dissimulāvī, dissimulātus	cover up, conceal
obscūrō, obscūrāre, obscūrāvī, obscūrātus	cover up, darken
occultō, occultāre, occultāvī, occultātus	hide

2nd Conjugation

lateō, latēre, latuī	lie hidden, be concealed

3rd Conjugation

abscondō, abscondere, abscondī, absconditus	hide, put out of sight
claudō, claudere, clausī, clausus	shut, close
condō, condere, condidī, conditus	hide, conceal, shut, bury
contegō, contegere, contēxī, contēctus	cover, roof, bury, hide
dēlitēscō (dēlitīscō), dēlitēscere, dēlituī	hide, conceal oneself, lurk
involvō, involvere, involvī, involūtus	cover completely, wrap up
obruō, obruere, obruī, obrutus	bury, hide, overwhelm
occulō, occulere, occuluī, occultus	hide, conceal, cover over
praetexō, praetexere, praetexuī, praetextus	disguise, cloak, pretend
recondō, recondere, recondidī, reconditus	lay up, put away, hoard, shut up, close, conceal, bury
sēclūdō, sēclūdere, sēclūsī, sēclūsus	shut off, shut up, seclude, hide, banish
tegō, tegere, tēxī, tēctus	cover, cover over, cloak, hide, conceal, keep secret

4th Conjugation

operiō, operīre, operuī, opertus	hide, clothe, bury
vestiō, vestīre, vestiī/vestīvī, vestītus	cover with a garment, clothe, cover, array, deck

• Confessing

Regular

3rd Conjugation

agnōscō, agnōscere, agnōvī, agnitus	own up, admit to, acknowledge

Deponent

2nd Conjugation

cōnfiteor, cōnfitērī, cōnfessus sum	confess, allow, acknowledge, avow
fateor, fatērī, fassus sum	grant, acknowledge, confess, own
profiteor, profitērī, professus sum	confess openly, profess, own freely, acknowledge

• DECIDING, JUDGING

Regular

1st Conjugation

dīiūdicō, dīiūdicāre, dīiūdicāvī, dīiūdicātus	judge, decide, determine, distinguish
iūdicō, iūdicāre, iūdicāvī, iūdicātus	judge, declare, decide, pass judgment

3rd Conjugation

cōnstituō, cōnstituere, cōnstituī, cōnstitūtus	define, decide, determine, decree, judge, arbitrate
dēcernō, dēcernere, dēcrēvī, dēcrētus	decide, determine, judge, decree, form a purpose, resolve
indūcō, indūcere, indūxī, inductus + in animum	determine, conclude, persuade oneself, resolve
statuō, statuere, statuī, statūtus	decide, determine, make a decision, be convinced, judge, conclude

• Desiring

Regular

1st Conjugation

anhēlō, anhēlāre, anhēlāvī, anhēlātus	breathe out, pant after
dēsīderō, dēsīderāre, dēsīderāvī, dēsīderātus	wish for, desire, expect, require, long for
optō, optāre, optāvī, optātus	wish, wish for, desire, pray for

2nd Conjugation

studeō, studēre, studuī	be eager, give attention to, desire, wish, apply oneself

3rd Conjugation

appetō, appetere, appetiī/appetīvī, appetītus	strive after, long for, desire, seek, court
concupīscō, concupīscere, concupiī/concupīvī, concupītus	long for, covet, be very desirous of, aspire to

3rd io Conjugation

cupiō, cupere, cupiī/cupīvī, cupītus	long for, desire, wish

Irregular

volō, velle, voluī	wish, want, will, purpose, be minded

• Destroying

Regular

1st Conjugation

prōflīgō, prōflīgāre, prōflīgāvī, prōflīgātus	ruin, destroy, crush, overthrow
spoliō, spoliāre, spoliāvī, spoliātus	pillage, despoil, rob, plunder
vastō, vastāre, vastāvī, vastātus	devastate, destroy, ravage, void, lay waste

2nd Conjugation

dēleō, dēlēre, dēlēvī, dēlētus	abolish, destroy, annihilate, raze, obliterate

3rd Conjugation

caedō, caedere, cecīdī, caesus	vanquish, destroy, beat, strike, chop, cut
cōnfringō, cōnfringere, cōnfrēgī, cōnfrāctus	break into pieces, shatter, destroy, crush
convellō, convellere, convellī (convulsī), convulsus	destroy, overthrow, nullify, dismember, tear to pieces
corrumpō, corrumpere, corrūpī, corruptus	destroy, ruin, waste
dēstruō, dēstruere, dēstruxī, dēstructus	destroy, ruin, demolish, tear down, raze
dīruō, dīruere, dīruī, dīrutus	overthrow, demolish, destroy
ēruō, ēruere, ēruī, ērutus	root out, destroy utterly
ēvertō, ēvertere, ēvertī, ēversus	destroy, overthrow, ruin, abolish
excīdō, excīdere, excīdī, excīsus	demolish, destroy, lay waste, cut down
exscindō, exscindere, exscidī, exscissus	annihilate, destroy, extirpate
exstinguō, exstinguere, exstīnxī, exstīnctus	abolish, destroy, annihilate, quench
interimō, interimere, interēmī, interemptus	destroy, abolish, take away, do away with

obruō, obruere, obruī, obrutus	destroy, cast down, overcome, overwhelm
percellō, percellere, perculī, perculsus	overthrow, ruin, destroy, beat down
perdō, perdere, perdidī, perditus	destroy, waste, ruin, squander, dissipate
prōterō, prōterere, prōtrīvī, prōtrītus	crush, destroy, overthrow, maltreat, tread under foot
rescindō, rescindere, rescidī, rescissus	abolish, abrogate, rescind, tear open
tollō, tollere, sustulī, sublātus	make away with, do away with, destroy, ruin
vertō, vertere, vertī, versus	overthrow, subvert, destroy

3rd io Conjugation

cōnficio, cōnficere, cōnfēcī, cōnfectus	destroy, sweep away, subdue, wear out
dīripiō, dīripere, dīripuī, dīreptus	lay waste, ravage, plunder, pillage, spoil

Deponent

1st Conjugation

praedor, praedārī, praedātus sum	ravish, plunder, spoil, make prey of

• Discovering

Regular

1st Conjugation

explōrō, explōrāre, explōrāvī, explōrātus — investigate, explore, search out

investīgō, investīgāre, investīgāvī, investīgātus — discover, investigate, find out, trace out

3rd Conjugation

cognōscō, cognōscere, cognōvī, cognitus — acquire knowledge of, inquire into, investigate

comprehendō, comprehendere, comprehendī, comprehensus — discover, detect, perceive

4th Conjugation

aperiō, aperīre, aperuī, apertus — discover, lay bare, uncover, reveal

comperiō, comperīre, comperī, compertus — discover, find out, obtain knowledge of

inveniō, invenīre, invēnī, inventus — discover, find out, ascertain, learn, come upon, invent

reperiō, reperīre, repperī, repertus — find again, find out, discover, learn, invent

• Doing

Regular

1st Conjugation

cōnflō, cōnflāre, cōnflāvī, cōnflātus — bring about, produce, cause, effect

occupō, occupāre, occupāvī, occupātus — do first, anticipate, get the start of

patrō, patrāre — bring to pass, execute, achieve, accomplish

perpetrō, perpetrāre, perpetrāvī, perpetrātus — achieve, execute, accomplish, carry through

3rd Conjugation

agō, agere, ēgī, āctus — put in motion, perform, do, transact

committō, committere, commīsī, commissus — carry on, wage, fight, practice, commit, do, be guilty of

contrahō, contrahere, contrāxī, contractus — bring about, execute, produce

gerō, gerere, gessī, gestus — do, perform, accomplish, manage

peragō, peragere, perēgī, perāctus — go through with, carry out, accomplish

solvō, solvere, solvī, solūtus — accomplish, fulfill, complete

trānsigō, trānsigere, trānsēgī, trānsāctus — carry through, finish, perform, transact

3rd io Conjugation

antecapiō, antecapere, antecēpī, anteceptus — take action beforehand, anticipate

faciō, facere, fēcī, factus — make, do, produce, perform, execute

perficiō, perficere, perfēcī, perfectus — bring about, cause, effect, finish

Deponent

1st Conjugation

versor, versārī, versātus sum — be engaged, occupy oneself, be employed

3rd Conjugation

dēfungor, dēfungī, dēfūnctus sum (+ abl) — perform, finish, be content with; die

fungor, fungī, fūnctus sum (+ abl) — perform, do, busy oneself, be engaged

Irregular

obeō, obīre, obiī/obīvī, obitus — engage in, undertake, execute, accomplish; die

• DYING

Regular

1st Conjugation

exspīrō, exspīrāre	expire, breathe one's last, perish

2nd Conjugation

iaceō, iacēre, iacuī, iacitum	lie dead, have fallen

3rd Conjugation

cadō, cadere, cecidī, cāsum	fall dead, die, be slain, perish, cease
conruō (corruō), conruere, conruī	fall down, die, perish, fall in ruin
dēcēdō, dēcēdere, dēcessī, dēcessum	die, depart, disappear, cease, retire
occidō, occidere, occidī, occāsum	fall, perish, die, be slain, be ruined
occumbō, occumbere, occubuī, occubitus	fall in death, die

Deponent

3rd Conjugation

dēfungor, dēfungī, dēfunctus sum	die
fungor, fungī, fūnctus sum + morte/fātō	die

3rd io Conjugation

ēmorior, ēmorī, ēmortuus sum	die, die off, decease, pass away
morior, morī, mortuus sum	die, expire, wither, die out

Irregular

dispereō, disperīre, disperiī	perish, be undone, go to ruin
intereō, interīre, interiī, interitum	die, decay, go to ruin, perish
obeō, obīre, obiī/obīvī, obitus	die
pereō, perīre, periī/perīvī, peritum	perish, pass away, die, lose life; pine away

• Embracing

Deponent

3rd Conjugation

amplector, amplectī, amplexus sum

embrace, encircle, comprehend, cling to

complector, complectī, complexus sum

embrace, clasp, grasp, encircle, grasp mentally

• ENTRUSTING

Regular

1st Conjugation

commendō, commendāre, commendāvī, commendātus — entrust, commit, confide

3rd Conjugation

committō, committere, commīsī, commissus — entrust (a person to…)

concrēdō, concrēdere, concrēdidī, concrēditus — entrust, confide (a secret)

cōnfīdō, cōnfīdere, cōnfīsus sum (+ dat) — trust, give trust

crēdō, crēdere, crēdidī, crēditus — entrust, trust

dēpōnō, dēpōnere, dēposuī, dēpositus (+ apud + acc) — entrust to, commit to the care of

permittō, permittere, permīsī, permissus — entrust, surrender, commit, grant

• Escaping

Regular

1st Conjugation

vītō, vītāre, vītāvī, vītātus	escape, avoid, evade

3rd Conjugation

ēlūdō, ēlūdere, ēlūsī, ēlūsus	avoid, elude, escape, shun, frustrate, mock
ēvādō, ēvādere, ēvāsī, ēvāsus	get away, escape, come away

3rd io Conjugation

dēfugiō, dēfugere, dēfūgī	shun, avoid, escape from, flee from, run off, make an escape
effugiō, effugere, effūgī	flee away, get away, escape, flee from, escape the notice of
fugiō, fugere, fūgī, fugitus	run away, flee, flee from, avoid, escape
profugiō, profugere, profūgī, profugitūrus	flee, run away, escape, take refuge
recipiō, recipere, recēpī, receptus + sē	withdraw, escape, retreat, draw back
refugiō, refugere, refūgī	flee back, flee for safety, avoid, shun

Deponent

3rd Conjugation

ēlābor, ēlābī, ēlāpsus sum	escape, slip away, glide off, get clear

· FALLING

Regular

3rd Conjugation

accidō, accidere, accidī	fall upon, fall to, fall before, fall at the feet
cadō, cadere, cecidī, cāsum	fall, fall down, descend, fall dead
concidō, concidere, concidī	fall together, fall down, tumble, fall to earth, fall dead
excidō, excidere, excidī	fall out, drop down, fall away, slip out, perish
incidō, incidere, incidī, incāsum	fall in, fall, find the way, reach, fall in with, come upon, fall out, happen
incumbō, incumbere, incubuī, incubitum (+ dat)	fall on, lean towards, overhang
occidō, occidere, occidī, occāsum	fall down, fall; go down, set; decline, end, perish
occumbō, occumbere, occubuī, occubitus	fall in death, die
recidō, recidere, recidī, recāsum	fall back, spring back, return, sink, relapse
ruō, ruere, ruī, rūtum	fall with violence, fall down, tumble down, go to ruin, fail, sink, be ruined

Deponent

3rd Conjugation

conlābor, conlābī, conlāpsus sum	fall together, fall, sink, fall in ruins, crumble
lābor, lābī, lāpsus sum	fall, sink, begin to fall, go to ruin, decline

• Fearing

Regular

1st Conjugation

formīdō, formīdāre, formīdāvī, formīdātus	fear, dread, be terrified, be afraid

2nd Conjugation

paveō, pavēre, pāvī	be in terror, tremble, quake with fear, be afraid, be terrified
timeō, timēre, timuī	fear, be afraid, dread

3rd Conjugation

expavēscō, expavēscere, expāvī	fear greatly, dread, be terrified
horrēscō, horrēscere, horruī	fear, dread, be terrified, shudder, begin to shake
metuō, metuere, metuī, metūtus	fear, be afraid, stand in fear
perhorrēscō, perhorrēscere, perhorruī	shake with terror, shudder
pertimēscō, pertimēscere, pertimuī	be alarmed, fear greatly, be frightened

Deponent

2nd Conjugation

vereor, verērī, veritus sum	fear, be afraid, dread, stand in awe

· FIGHTING

Regular

1st Conjugation

bellō, bellāre, bellāvī, bellātum	wage war, war, fight
certō, certāre, certāvī, certātus	combat, do battle, struggle, contend, compete
dēpugnō, dēpugnāre, dēpugnāvī, dēpugnātus	fight out, join battle, combat, quarrel
dīmicō, dīmicāre, dīmicāvī, dīmicātus	fight, contend, struggle, be in conflict
expugnō, expugnāre, expugnāvī, expugnātus	take by assault, storm
oppugnō, oppugnāre, oppugnāvī, oppugnātus	fight against, attack, storm, besiege
pugnō, pugnāre, pugnāvī, pugnātus	fight, combat, engage, contend
repugnō, repugnāre, repugnāvī, repugnātus (+ dat)	fight back, oppose, resist, struggle

2nd Conjugation

moveō, movēre, mōvī, mōtus + arma	attack, give battle

3rd Conjugation

committō, committere, commīsī, commissus	fight, carry on, wage
concurrō, concurrere, concurrī, concursum	fight, engage in combat
cōnflīgō, cōnflīgere, cōnflīxī, cōnflictus	fight, combat, contend, be at war
contendō, contendere, contendī, contentus	lay siege to, fight, contend, dispute
gerō, gerere, gessī, gestus + bellum	fight, wage war
lacessō, lacessere, lacessīvī, lacessītus	provoke, challenge, attack
petō, petere, petiī/petīvī, petītus	attack, assault, fly at, aim at

Deponent

1st Conjugation

dēproelior, dēproeliārī — war violently

luctor, luctārī, luctātus sum — strive, contend, wrestle, struggle

proelior, proeliārī, proeliātus sum — engage in battle, fight, join battle

3rd Conjugation

īnsequor, īnsequī, īnsecūtus sum — keep striking

ulcīscor, ulcīscī, ultus sum — avenge, punish, take vengeance on

3rd io Conjugation

aggredior, aggredī, aggressus sum — attack, assault

4th Conjugation

adorior, adorīrī, adortus sum — attack, assail, fall upon

• Flourishing

Regular

2nd Conjugation

aveō, avēre	be well, fare well, be happy
flōreō, flōrēre, flōruī	flourish, be prosperous, flower
salveō, salvēre	be well, be in good health
valeō, valēre, valuī, valitūrus	be strong, be well, succeed
vigeō, vigēre, viguī	flourish, be vigorous, be strong, be lively

3rd Conjugation

florēscō, florēscere, florēscuī	begin to bloom, increase in renown
nitēscō, nitēscere, nitēscuī	begin to thrive
succēdō, succēdere, successī, successus	succeed, be successful, prosper, go on well
vīvēscō, vīvēscere	grow lively, get full of life

• FOLLOWING

Regular

1st Conjugation

comitō, comitāre, comitāvī, comitātus — follow, attend, accompany

3rd Conjugation

succēdō, succēdere, successī, successus — follow, follow after, take the place of, succeed

3rd io Conjugation

excipiō, excipere, excēpī, exceptus — follow, succeed, catch up

Deponent

1st Conjugation

adsector, adsectārī, adsectātus sum — follow, wait upon

sector, sectārī, sectātus sum — follow eagerly, run after, chase, pursue

3rd Conjugation

adsequor, adsequī, adsecūtus sum — follow up, overtake, pursue

cōnsequor, cōnsequī, cōnsecūtus sum — follow, follow up, go after, pursue, overtake, copy, imitate

īnsequor, īnsequī, īnsecūtus sum — follow, follow after, come next, succeed, press upon, pursue

obsequor, obsequī, obsecūtus sum — comply with, yield to

prōsequor, prōsequī, prōsecūtus sum — follow, attend, escort, accompany, pursue

sequor, sequī, secūtus sum — follow, come after, attend, accompany, pursue

• Forcing

Regular

3rd Conjugation

cōgō, cōgere, coēgī, coāctus	force, drive, press, compel, urge, constrain
compellō, compellere, compulī, compulsus	force, drive, impel, incite, urge, compel
ingerō, ingerere, ingessī, ingestus (+ dat)	force on (someone)
perrumpō, perrumpere, perrūpī, perruptus	force one's way through
rumpō, rumpere, rūpī, ruptus	force, make by force, burst

Deponent

1st Conjugation

ēluctor, ēluctārī, ēluctātus sum	force a way out

• FOUNDING

Regular

1st Conjugation

fundō, fundāre, fundāvī, fundātus	found, establish, secure

3rd Conjugation

condō, condere, condidī, conditus	found, establish, build, settle
cōnstituō, cōnstituere, cōnstituī, cōnstitūtus	found, fix, erect, set up, construct, establish
dēdūcō, dēdūcere, dēdūxī, dēductus	found a colony, lead forth, conduct
sistō, sistere, stitī/stetī, status	establish, cause to stand, confirm, set up, fix, plant

• GAINING, GETTING, ACQUIRING

Regular

1st Conjugation

comparō, comparāre, comparāvī, comparātus	get, procure, purchase, obtain
conciliō, conciliāre, conciliāvī, conciliātus	procure, gain, acquire, obtain
impetrō, impetrāre, impetrāvī, impetrātus	gain one's end, get, obtain, achieve, procure (by request or influence)
parō, parāre, parāvī, parātus	procure, get, obtain, acquire, buy

2nd Conjugation

obtineō, obtinēre, obtinuī, obtentus	get possession of, acquire, obtain, gain

3rd Conjugation

adquīrō, adquīrere, adquīsīvī, adquīsītus	obtain, gain, win, get in addition, obtain besides, accumulate

3rd io Conjugation

pariō, parere, peperī, partus	procure, acquire, obtain, devise, invent

Deponent

3rd Conjugation

adipīscor, adipīscī, adeptus sum	attain, get, acquire, obtain, reach
adsequor, adsequī, adsecūtus sum	gain, reach, attain, effect
cōnsequor, cōnsequī, cōnsecūtus sum	attain to, arrive at, reach, obtain, get, acquire
nancīscor, nancīscī, nactus/nānctus sum	get, obtain, light upon, reach, find

4th Conjugation

potior, potīrī, potītus sum   get, obtain, acquire, become
                                               master of, take possession
                                               of, usurp supreme
                                               authority

• Gathering, Collecting

Regular

1st Conjugation

adgregō (aggregō), adgregāre, adgregāvī, adgregātus — collect, bring together, bring together in a flock

comparō, comparāre, comparāvī, comparātus — bring together as equals, pair, match

congregō, congregāre, congregāvī, congregātus — collect, assemble, collect in a flock, swarm

3rd Conjugation

carpō, carpere, carpsī, carptus — gather, pluck, crop, pick, pluck off

cōgō, cōgere, coēgī, coāctus — collect, convene, bring together, congregate

condūcō, condūcere, condūxī, condūctus — gather, collect, unite, assemble, hire, employ

coniungō, coniungere, coniūnxī, coniūnctus — gather, unite, connect, join

conligō (colligō), conligere, collēgī, collēctus — gather, collect, assemble, bring together

contrahō, contrahere, contrāxī, contractus — draw together, collect, assemble, draw close, draw in, contract

legō, legere, lēgī, lēctus — gather, collect, bring together, choose, pick out, appoint

3rd io Conjugation

percipiō, percipere, percēpī, perceptus — get, collect, obtain, take wholly, take to oneself, comprehend

4th Conjugation

acciō, accīre, accīvī, accītus	summon, invite
conveniō, convenīre, convēnī, conventus	gather, assemble, come together, meet

Irregular

cōnferō, cōnferre, cōntulī, cōnlātus	bring together, collect, gather, bring together in thought

• GIVING

Regular

1st Conjugation

dō, dare, dedī, datus	give, bestow, grant, confer
dōnō, dōnāre, dōnāvī, dōnātus	bestow, grant, give as a present, gift, pardon
lēgō, lēgāre, lēgāvī, lēgātus	bequeath, leave by will

2nd Conjugation

praebeō, praebēre, praebuī, praebitus	give, grant, furnish, supply, offer

3rd Conjugation

attribuō, attribuere, attribuī, attribūtus	give, bestow, assign, allot, confer
oppōnō, oppōnere, opposuī, oppositus	set before, present, bring forward
pangō, pangere, pepigī/pānxī/pēgī, pāctus	promise in marriage, betroth, dedicate
reddō, reddere, reddidī, redditus	give back, return, give up and over, deliver, give, assign, surrender, relinquish
tribuō, tribuere, tribuī, tribūtus	grant, give, bestow, impart, allot, pay

3rd io Conjugation

sufficiō, sufficere, suffēcī, suffectus	give, supply

4th Conjugation

impertiō, impertīre	give, assign, direct, bestow, impart, give a part, share with

Deponent

4th Conjugation

largior, largīrī, largītus sum	give bountifully, lavish, distribute, bestow, be generous

Irregular

dēferō, dēferre, dētulī, dēlātus	give, grant, bring, confer, allot, offer, deliver
offerō, offerre, obtulī, oblātus	bring, present, offer, confer, bestow

• Going

Regular

1st Conjugation

comitō, comitāre, comitāvī, comitātus	accompany, follow, attend
dēmigrō, dēmigrāre, dēmigrāvī, dēmigrātus	go away, depart, migrate, move

3rd Conjugation

accēdō, accēdere, accessī, accessum	go to, come to, come near, approach
cēdō, cēdere, cessī, cessus	go from, go away, depart, abandon, drop out, yield to
concēdō, concēdere, concessī, concessus	go away, give way, depart, retire, withdraw, yield, submit
dēcēdō, dēcēdere, dēcessī, dēcessum	go away, retreat, make way, withdraw
intendō, intendere, intendī, intentus/ intensus + iter	direct one's march, reach out, extend
prōcēdō, prōcēdere, prōcessī, prōcessum	go before, go forward, advance, proceed, march on, move forward
prōdūcō, prōdūcere, prōdūxī, prōductus	lead forth, advance, promote
vādō, vādere, vāsī	go, walk, go hastily, proceed rapidly, rush

4th Conjugation

ambiō, ambīre, ambiī/ambīvī, ambitus	go round, go about, surround, encircle

Deponent

1st Conjugation

peregrīnor, peregrīnārī, peregrīnātus sum	go abroad, travel about, roam, wander, be a stranger, sojourn in a strange land

3rd Conjugation

proficīscor, proficīscī, profectus sum	set forward, set out, go, march, depart

3rd io Conjugation

adgredior, adgredī, adgressus sum	approach, go against, fall upon
ēgredior, ēgredī, ēgressus sum	go out, come forth, march out, go away
prōgredior, prōgredī, prōgressus sum	go forward, advance, proceed, go on

Irregular

adeō, adīre, adiī/adīvī, aditus	go to, come to, come up to, approach
cōnferō, cōnferre, cōntulī, cōnlātus + sē	devote oneself, apply, go
eō, īre, iī/īvī, itum	go, walk, ride, march, move, advance, proceed, go about
prōdeō, prōdīre, prōdiī, proditum	go forth, come forth, come forward
redeō, redīre, rediī, reditum	go back, turn back, return

• GUARDING

Regular

1st Conjugation

adservō, adservāre, adservāvī, adservātus	watch over, guard, preserve
cūrō, cūrāre, cūrāvī, cūrātus	care for, attend to, preside over
prōcūrō, prōcūrāre, prōcūrāvī, prōcūrātus	take care of, manage, attend to
servō, servāre, servāvī, servātus	make safe, guard, preserve, protect

2nd Conjugation

praesideō, praesidēre, praesēdī	guard, protect, watch, defend, superintend

4th Conjugation

custōdiō, custōdīre, custōdiī/custōdīvī, custodītus	watch, defend, guard, protect, keep, hold in custody, hold captive
mūniō, mūnīre, mūniī/mūnīvī, mūnītus	defend with a wall, fortify, defend, guard, secure, protect

Deponent

2nd Conjugation

tueor, tuērī, tutus/tuitus sum	watch over, care for, support, guard, preserve, defend, protect

• GUIDING

Regular

1st Conjugation

administrō, administrāre, administrāvī, administrātus

guide, direct, manage, control, rule

2nd Conjugation

doceō, docēre, docuī, doctus

teach, make aware, instruct

3rd Conjugation

dērigō, dērigere, dērēxī, dērēctus

guide, direct, limit, regulate, aim

dūcō, dūcere, dūxī, ductus

guide, lead, conduct, direct, escort

Deponent

1st Conjugation

moderor, moderārī, moderātus sum

guide, govern, rule, direct, set bounds, mitigate, temper, restrain

• Happening, Occurring

Regular

3rd Conjugation

accidō, accidere, accidī	come to pass, happen, occur, take place
cadō, cadere, cecidī, casum	happen, fall to the lot of, come to pass, occur, turn out
contingō, contingere, contigī, contāctus	happen, befall, take place, occur, come to pass
exsistō, exsistere, exstitī, exstitum	become, arise, be produced
incidō, incidere, incidī, incāsum	happen, occur, fall out, break out
intercēdō, intercēdere, intercessī, intercessum	occur, happen, come to pass

4th Conjugation

ēveniō, ēvenīre, ēvēnī, ēventum	happen, befall, come to pass
veniō, venīre, vēnī, ventum	occur, happen, result, come

Irregular

fīō, fierī, factus sum	become, be turned into, be made

• Having

Regular	
2nd Conjugation	
habeō, habēre, habuī, habitus	have, hold, support, carry, wear, possess
obtineō, obtinēre, obtinuī, obtentus	have, possess, hold fast, preserve, keep
teneō, tenēre, tenuī, tentus	hold, keep, have, grasp, hold fast
3rd Conjugation	
gerō, gerere, gessī, gestus	have, contain

Deponent	
3rd Conjugation	
ūtor, ūtī, ūsus sum (+ two ablatives)	use as, have, employ for, hold in the capacity of

Irregular	
sum, esse, fuī, futurus (+ dat of possession)	have

• Hearing

Regular

1st Conjugation

auscultō, auscultāre, auscultāvī, auscultātus — listen, listen to, overhear

3rd Conjugation

attendō, attendere, attendī, attentus — listen to

3rd io Conjugation

excipiō, excipere, excēpī, exceptus — listen to, overhear

4th Conjugation

audiō, audīre, audiī/audīvī, audītus — hear, listen to

exaudiō, exaudīre, exaudiī/exaudīvī, exaudītus — hear clearly, discern, hear, attend to, regard

inaudiō, inaudīre, inaudīvī, inaudītus — hear, get wind of, learn

• HELPING

Regular

1st Conjugation

adiuvō, adiuvāre, adiūvī, adiūtus	help, assist, sustain, aid
administrō, administrāre, administrāvī, administrātus	assist, manage
iuvō, iuvāre, iūvī, iūtus	help, aid, assist, serve, support

3rd Conjugation

succurrō, succurrere, succurrī, succursum (+ dat)	run to help, hasten to the aid of, help, aid, assist

4th Conjugation

subveniō, subvenīre, subvēnī, subventum	come to help, aid, assist, reinforce, relieve

Deponent

1st Conjugation

auxilior, auxiliārī, auxiliātus sum	give help, aid, assist
opitulor, opitulārī, opitulātus sum (+ dat)	bring aid, help, assist, aid

Irregular

adsum, adesse, adfuī, adfutūrus	help, aid, support
prōsum, prōdesse, prōfuī, prōfutūrus	be of use, serve

• HESITATING

Regular

1st Conjugation

aestuō, aestuāre, aestuāvī, aestuātum	waver, hesitate, be in doubt, vacillate
dubitō, dubitāre, dubitāvī, dubitātus	hesitate, delay, waver, be in doubt, doubt
haesitō, haesitāre, haesitāvī, haesitātum	hesitate, be at a loss
trepidō, trepidāre, trepidāvī, trepidātus	hesitate, waver, tremble, be at a loss

2nd Conjugation

haereō, haerēre, haesī, haesum	hesitate, be embarrassed, be perplexed, be at a loss

3rd Conjugation

ambigō, ambigere	hesitate, waver, be in doubt, doubt

Deponent

1st Conjugation

cunctor, cunctārī, cunctātus sum	hesitate, delay, linger, doubt
flūctuor, flūctuārī, flūctuātus sum	hesitate, be in doubt, waver
moror, morārī, morātus sum	delay, wait, linger, remain

• HURRYING

Regular

1st Conjugation

accelerō, accelerāre, accelerāvī, accelerātus	make haste
dēproperō, dēproperāre	hasten, prepare hastily
festīnō, festīnāre, festīnāvī, festīnātus	hasten, make haste, hurry, do speedily
mātūrō, mātūrāre, mātūrāvī, mātūrātus	make haste, hasten, accelerate, quicken, expedite
properō, properāre, properāvī, properātus	make haste, hasten, be quick, go quickly, be in haste, prepare with haste
trepidō, trepidāre, trepidāvī, trepidātus	hurry with alarm

3rd Conjugation

concurrō, concurrere, concurrī, concursum	make haste, run for help
contendō, contendere, contendī, contentus	hasten, exert oneself
currō, currere, cucurrī, cursus	hasten, move quickly, run
inruō, inruere, inruī	rush in, rush into
recurrō, recurrere, recurrī, recursum	hasten back, run back, return
ruō, ruere, ruī, rutus	hurry, hasten, rush, dash, run

3rd io Conjugation

corripiō, corripere, corripuī, correptus	hurry over, make haste over, quicken

• Joining

Regular

1st Conjugation

cōnsociō, cōnsociāre, cōnsociāvī, cōnsociātus	join, unite, connect, share
continuō, continuāre, continuāvī, continuātus	join together, connect, make continuous

3rd Conjugation

addō, addere, addidī, additus	join, bring to, add to
adiungō, adiungere, adiūnxī, adiūnctus	join to, fasten to, add, join, associate, annex, attach
committō, committere, commīsī, commissus	join, combine, bring together, unite, connect
cōnectō, cōnectere, cōnexuī, cōnexus	join, connect, bind together, unite, link, compose
iungō, iungere, iūnxī, iūnctus	join, join together

Irregular

intersum, interesse, interfuī	be present, take part; (+ dat) take part in

• Killing

Regular

1st Conjugation

exanimō, exanimāre, exanimāvī, exanimātus — fatigue, deprive of life, kill, wear out

mactō, mactāre, mactāvī, mactātus — offer sacrifice, immolate, kill, slaughter, put to death

necō, necāre, necāvī, necātus — kill, put to death, slay

trucīdō, trucīdāre — slaughter, butcher, massacre, cut to pieces

3rd Conjugation

concīdō, concīdere, concīdī, concīsus — kill, cut up, cut to pieces, ruin, destroy

cōnscīscō, cōnscīscere, cōnscīvī, cōnscītus + sibi mortem — commit suicide

exstinguō, exstinguere, exstīnxī, exstīnctus — deprive of life, kill, destroy, annihilate, abolish, quench

interimō, interimere, interēmī, interemptus — destroy, kill, slay

occīdō, occīdere, occīdī, occīsus — kill, slay, cut off, cut down

3rd io Conjugation

cōnficiō, cōnficere, cōnfēcī, cōnfectus — kill, subdue, diminish, destroy, weaken, wear out, consume

dēiciō, dēicere, dēiēcī, dēiectus — kill, slay, slaughter, strike down

interficiō, interficere, interfēcī, interfectus — kill, murder, slay, put out of the way; (with sē: commit suicide)

percutiō, percutere, percussī, percussus — slay, kill

• KNOWING

Regular

1st Conjugation

nōscitō, nōscitāre, nōscitāvī, nōscitātus — know, recognize, perceive, observe

2nd Conjugation

calleō, callēre, calluī — have the knowledge of, know by experience, be skilled, know how

3rd Conjugation

cognōscō, cognōscere, cognōvī, cognitus — acquire knowledge of, learn, ascertain, perceive; (in perfect tense: know)

intellegō, intellegere, intellēxī, intellēctus — to come to know, perceive, understand, be master of

nōscō, nōscere, nōvī, nōtus — come to know, get knowledge of, learn, become acquainted with

nōvī - perfect stem — know, understand, have learned

3rd io Conjugation

percipiō, percipere, percēpī, perceptus — know, learn, comprehend, conceive, understand, perceive

4th Conjugation

sciō, scīre, sciī/scīvī, scītus — know, understand, perceive, have knowledge of, be skilled in

sentiō, sentīre, sēnsī, sēnsus — discern by sense, perceive, feel, understand, notice

• LEADING

Regular	

3rd Conjugation

addūcō, addūcere, addūxī, adductus	lead to, bring to, bring along, lead, persuade
attrahō, attrahere, attrāxī, attrāctus	lead, draw, allure
dēdūcō, dēdūcere, dēdūxī, dēdūctus	lead away, lead off, conduct, escort, accompany
dērigō, dērigere, dērēxī, dērēctus	steer, drive, direct, guide
dūcō, dūcere, dūxī, ductus	lead, conduct, draw, bring, cause to move, march, move, incite
ēdūcō, ēdūcere, ēdūxī, ēductus	lead forth, draw out, march out, conduct, bring up, rear
intrōdūcō, intrōdūcere, intrōdūxī, intrōductus	lead in, bring in, introduce, admit, bring forward
perdūcō, perdūcere, perdūxī, perductus	lead through, lead, conduct, bring, prolong, guide, win over
regō, regere, rēxī, rēctus	lead aright, guide, control, lead, conduct

Irregular	
praesum, praeesse, praefuī, praefutūrus (+ dat)	preside over, have charge of, be before, rule, take the lead

• LEARNING

Regular

1st Conjugation

scīscitō, scīscitāre (with dē + abl)	ask about

3rd Conjugation

cognōscō, cognōscere, cognōvī, cognitus	learn, perceive, understand, become acquainted with, acquire knowledge of
dēprehendō, dēprehendere, dēprehendī, dēprehensus	find out, discover, detect, observe, comprehend, understand
discō, discere, didicī	learn, become acquainted with, learn to know
intellegō, intellegere, intellēxī, intellēctus	come to know, comprehend, understand
nōscō, nōscere, nōvī, nōtus	learn, discern, come to know, get knowledge of
perdiscō, perdiscere, perdidicī	learn thoroughly, learn by heart

3rd io Conjugation

percipiō, percipere, percēpī, perceptus	learn, know, comprehend, understand, perceive
perspiciō, perspicere, perspexī, perspectus	look closely at, perceive clearly, discern, observe, contemplate

Deponent

1st Conjugation

scīscitor, scīscitārī, scīscitātus sum	seek to know, ask, inquire, inform oneself

• LEAVING

Regular

1st Conjugation

dēmigrō, dēmigrāre, dēmigrāvī, dēmigrātum	depart, go away, migrate, emigrate

3rd Conjugation

dēscīscō, dēscīscere, dēscīvī, dēscītum	depart, deviate, withdraw, desert, be unfaithful, leave; (with ā vitā: kill oneself)
dēserō, dēsere, dēseruī, dēsertus	leave, forsake, abandon, desert, give up
dēstituō, dēstituere, dēstituī, dēstitūtus	leave, abandon, desert, forsake, leave alone
discēdō, discēdere, discessī, discessum	go away, leave, depart, give up, abandon
excēdō, excēdere, excessī, excessus	depart, go forth, withdraw, leave, disappear
linquō, linquere, līquī	leave, go away, forsake, depart from
relinquō, relinquere, relīquī, relictus	leave behind, leave, not stay with, not take along, abandon

3rd io Conjugation

dēficiō, dēficere, dēfēcī, dēfectus	leave, desert, fail, abandon, withdraw, depart
fugiō, fugere, fūgī, fugitus	leave the country, flee, flee from, go into exile

Deponent

3rd Conjugation

proficīscor, proficīscī, profectus sum	depart, march, set out

3rd io Conjugation

dīgredior, dīgredī, dīgressus sum	depart, go away, digress
ēgredior, ēgredī, ēgressus sum	go away, march out, go out

Irregular

abeō, abīre, abiī, abitum	depart, go away, go from, go forth
exeō, exīre, exiī/exīvī, exitus	depart, withdraw, go out, go forth, go away, retire

• LIVING

Regular

1st Conjugation

habitō, habitāre, habitāvī, habitātus — live, abide, reside, dwell

3rd Conjugation

agō, agere, ēgī, āctus — live, pass time, be; (with vītam: lead one's life)

colō, colere, coluī, cultus — live, dwell, inhabit, stay in

incolō, incolere, incoluī — abide, dwell, inhabit, be at home

vīvō, vīvere, vīxī, victum — live, have life, be alive, survive

---

Deponent

1st Conjugation

rūsticor, rūsticārī, rūsticātus sum — live in the country, stay in the country

versor, versārī, versātus sum — dwell, live, abide

• Losing

Regular

1st Conjugation

aliēnō, aliēnāre, aliēnāvī, aliēnātus | lose, give up, part with

3rd Conjugation

āmittō, āmittere, āmīsī, āmissus | lose, part with, let go, let slip

perdō, perdere, perdidī, perditus | lose utterly, squander, throw away, waste

Deponent

1st Conjugation

perīclitor, perīclitārī, perīclitātus sum (+ abl) | be in danger of losing

• LOVING

Regular

1st Conjugation

amō, amāre, amāvī, amātus — love, like, find pleasure in

3rd Conjugation

colō, colere, coluī, cultus — love, honor, esteem, cherish

dīligō, dīligere, dīlēxī, dīlēctus — love, value, esteem, prize, appreciate

Deponent

1st Conjugation

amplexor, amplexārī, amplexātus sum — be fond of, value, esteem, embrace

3rd Conjugation

amplector, amplectī, amplexus sum — embrace, value, honor, embrace with love, esteem

Irregular

depereō, deperīre, deperīvī/deperiī — be hopelessly in love with

• Making, Producing, Creating

Regular

1st Conjugation

creō, creāre, creāvī, creātus — make, produce, create, beget, bring forth

generō, generāre, generāvī, generātus — produce, create, beget, engender

3rd Conjugation

exprimō, exprimere, expressī, expressus — form, model, portray, make, produce, express

fingō, fingere, finxī, fictus — invent, form, fashion, make, mould, give character to

gignō, gignere, genuī, genitus — produce, give birth to, beget

reddō, reddere, reddidī, redditus — make to be, cause to appear, make, render

redigō, redigere, redēgī, redāctus (with two accusatives) — make, render, cause to be

3rd io Conjugation

efficiō, efficere, effēcī, effectus — make, form, execute, finish, effect, cause

faciō, facere, fēcī, factus — make, construct, produce, compose, bring about

pariō, parere, peperī, partus — produce, create, invent, bear, give birth

Deponent

3rd Conjugation

comminīscor, comminīscī, commentus sum — invent, devise, contrive, feign

• MARCHING

Regular

3rd Conjugation

incēdō, incēdere, incessī, incessum	march, advance, stalk, strut, make way
pergō, pergere, perrēxī, perrēctus	march, go forward, make haste, hasten

3rd io Conjugation

faciō, facere, fēcī, factus + iter	march, take a trip

Irregular

eō, īre, iī/īvī, itum	march, move, advance, go (against an enemy)

• MEETING

Regular

3rd Conjugation

cōnflīgō, cōnflīgere, cōnflīxī, cōnflīctus	meet in combat, clash
occurrō, occurrere, occurrī, occursum	run to meet, meet
oppetō, oppetere, oppetiī/oppetīvī, oppetītus	go to meet, encounter

4th Conjugation

conveniō, convenīre, convēnī, conventus	meet, assemble, visit, come together, come in a body

Deponent

3rd io Conjugation

congredior, congredī, congressus sum	meet, come together, engage, contend

Irregular

coeō, coīre, coiī/coīvī, coitus	meet, come together, assemble, go together, ally oneself
obeō, obīre, obiī/obīvī, obitus	go to meet, visit
sum, esse, fuī, futūrus + obvius	meet, encounter
sum, esse, fuī, futūrus + praestō	meet, be in the way, resist, oppose

• MOURNING

Regular

1st Conjugation

dēplōrō, dēplōrāre, dēplōrāvī, dēplōrātus	weep bitterly, wail, lament, moan
inlacrimō (illacrimō), inlacrimāre, inlacrimāvī (+ dat)	weep over, bewail, lament, sorrow for
lacrimō/lacrumō, lacrimāre, lacrimāvī, lacrimātus	weep, shed tears, lament, bewail

2nd Conjugation

dēfleō, dēflēre, dēflēvī, dēflētus	weep over, lament, deplore, bewail
doleō, dolēre, doluī, dolitūrus	suffer, grieve, deplore, lament
fleō, flēre, flēvī, flētus	weep, cry, shed tears, lament, wail
lūgeō, lūgēre, lūxī, lūctus	mourn, lament, bewail, be in mourning, wear mourning apparel
maereō, maerēre	mourn, grieve, lament, be sad

3rd Conjugation

gemō, gemere, gemuī, gemitus	lament, sigh, groan, bewail, moan
requīrō, requīrere, requīsiī/requīsīvī, requīsītus	lament, lament the absence of

Deponent

1st Conjugation

lāmentor, lāmentārī, lāmentātus sum	wail, moan, weep, lament, bewail, bemoan

3rd Conjugation

queror, querī, questus sum	express grief, complain, lament, bewail

• Naming, Calling

Regular

1st Conjugation

appellō, appellāre, appellāvī, appellātus	call by name, name, address, call upon
dēmōnstrō, dēmonstrāre, dēmonstrāvī, dēmonstrātus	name, describe, speak of, mention
memorō, memorāre, memorāvī, memorātus	name, call, bring to remembrance
nōminō, nōmināre, nōmināvī, nōminātus	call by name, name, give a name to, render famous
nuncupō, nuncupāre, nuncupāvī, nuncupātus	call by name, name, call, proclaim formally
vocō, vocāre, vocāvī, vocātus	call, summon, call together, call upon

• OPENING, BEING OPEN, REVEALING

Regular

1st Conjugation

nūdō, nūdāre, nūdāvī, nūdātus	uncover, strip, lay bare, explain

2nd Conjugation

pateō, patēre, patuī	lie open, be open, stand open

3rd Conjugation

reclūdō, reclūdere, reclūsī, reclūsus	unclose, disclose, reveal, open, expose

3rd io Conjugation

facio, facere, fēcī, factus + palam	make public, make well known
patefaciō, patefacere, patefēcī, patefactus	open, throw open, lay open, disclose, expose

4th Conjugation

aperiō, aperīre, aperuī, apertus	uncover, lay bare, open, make visible

Irregular

sum, esse, fuī, futūrus + palam	be well known, be public

• Ordering, Commanding

Regular

1st Conjugation

cūrō, cūrare, cūrāvī, cūrātus (+ acc and gerundive)	order, see to, have done
dēnūntiō, dēnūntiāre, dēnūntiāvī, dēnūntiātus	order, threaten, direct, command
imperō, imperāre, imperāvī, imperātus	command, order, give an order, exercise authority
mandō, mandāre, mandāvī, mandātus	order, command, send word
nūntiō, nūntiāre, nūntiāvī, nūntiātus	give orders, direct, carry commands

2nd Conjugation

iubeō, iubēre, iussī, iūssus	order, command, give orders, decree

3rd Conjugation

regō, regere, rēxī, rēctus	rule, govern, be master of, control

3rd io Conjugation

faciō, facere, fēcī, factus + certiorem and ut/ne	order
praecipiō, praecipere, praecēpī, praeceptus	order, give rules, direct, admonish

• Placing

Regular	
1st Conjugation	
aptō, aptāre, aptāvī, aptātus	adapt, fit
collocō, collocāre, collocāvī, collocātus	place, set right, arrange, put, set, station
locō, locāre, locāvī, locātus	place, put, lay, set, arrange
3rd Conjugation	
dēpōnō, dēpōnere, dēposuī, dēpositus	put aside, set down, place, lay, set, deposit
impōnō, impōnere, imposuī, impositus	place upon, set on, place, introduce, establish
pōnō, pōnere, posuī, positus	place, put, set, put down, set down, fix
repōnō, repōnere, reposuī, repositus	put back, set back, lay aside, lay down, put away, place
3rd io Conjugation	
subiciō, subicere, subiēcī, subiectus	place under, make subject

• Praising

Regular

1st Conjugation

celebrō, celebrāre, celebrāvī, celebrātus	praise, honor, celebrate with praise, celebrate in song
collaudō, collaudāre, collaudāvī, collaudātus	extol, prize highly
decorō, decorāre, decorāvī, decorātus	honor, embellish, distinguish
laudō, laudāre, laudāvī, laudātus	praise, laud, commend, honor, extol
praedicō, praedicāre, praedicāvī, praedicātus	praise, recommend

3rd Conjugation

extollō, extollere	praise, laud, extol

Irregular

efferō, efferre, extūlī, ēlātus	praise, extol, promote
ferō, ferre, tulī, lātus	celebrate, extol, report

• Praying

Regular

1st Conjugation

adōrō, adōrāre, adōrāvī, adōrātus	worship, reverence, call upon, entreat, supplicate
ōrō, ōrāre, ōrāvī, ōrātus	pray, entreat, supplicate

2nd Conjugation

dēvoveō, dēvovēre, dēvōvī, dēvōtus	vow, devote, offer, sacrifice

3rd Conjugation

cōnstituō, cōnstituere, cōnstituī, cōnstitūtus	(Figuratively) worship; (Literally) decide, establish
extollō, extollere	exalt, extol, lift up, elevate

Deponent

1st Conjugation

dēprecor, dēprecārī, dēprecātus sum	avert by prayer, plead against, solicit, pray, pray for, intercede in behalf of
precor, precārī, precātus sum	pray, ask, call upon
veneror, venerārī, venerātus sum	worship, adore, revere, venerate, do homage to, ask reverently

• RAGING

Regular

1st Conjugation

aestuō, aestuāre, aestuāvī, aestuātum   rage, burn, be excited, be inflamed

3rd Conjugation

furō, furere   rage, rave, be furious, be out of one's mind, be madly in love with

4th Conjugation

saeviō, saevīre, saeviī, saevītum   be furious, be brutal, be violent, be savage

Deponent

1st Conjugation

indignor, indignārī, indignātus sum   be angry at, be offended, despise

īrāscor, īrāscārī   be in a rage, be angry

stomachor, stomachārī, stomachātus sum   be angry, fume, fret

• Receiving

Regular

1st Conjugation

aggregō, aggregāre, aggregāvī, aggregātus   assemble

3rd Conjugation

admittō, admittere, admīsī, admissus   let in, admit

adquīrō, adquīrere, adquīsīvī, adquīsītus   accumulate, obtain besides

ascīscō, ascīscere, ascīvī, ascītus   receive, admit, hire

ascrībō, ascrībere, ascrīpsī, ascrīptus   add, enroll, register

3rd io Conjugation

accipiō, accipere, accēpī, acceptus   receive, take without effort, accept

concipiō, concipere, concēpī, conceptus   receive, take hold of, take up, take in, conceive, become pregnant, perceive

excipiō, excipere, excēpī, exceptus   receive, capture, take, obtain, incur, meet

recipiō, recipere, recēpī, receptus   receive again, recover, repossess, admit, accept, welcome

• Rejoicing

Regular	
1st Conjugation	
exsultō, exsultāre, exsultāvī	exult, rejoice exceedingly, revel, jump up
2nd Conjugation	
gaudeō, gaudēre, gavīsus sum	rejoice, be glad, be joyful
pergaudeō, pergaudēre	be very glad
4th Conjugation	
gestiō, gestīre, gestiī/gestīvī	exult, be joyful, be delighted, gesticulate, express strong feeling, leap

Deponent	
1st Conjugation	
grātor, grātārī, grātātus sum	rejoice, rejoice with, manifest joy, congratulate, wish joy
grātulor, grātulārī, grātulātus sum	rejoice, manifest joy, be glad, congratulate
laetor, laetārī, laetātus sum	rejoice, be glad, be delighted
3rd Conjugation	
fruor, fruī, frūctus sum (+ abl)	derive enjoyment from, delight in
perfruor, perfruī, perfrūctus sum (+ abl)	be delighted, enjoy fully

• Remembering

Regular

1st Conjugation

commemorō, commemorāre, commemorāvī, commemorātus	recall to memory, call to mind, be mindful of, keep in mind, remember, bring to mind
memorō, memorāre, memorāvī, memorātus	bring to remembrance, recount

2nd Conjugation

habeō, habēre, habuī, habitus + memoriā	remember
teneō, tenēre, tenuī, tentus + memoriā	remember

3rd Conjugation

recognōscō, recognōscere, recognōvī, recognitus	recall to mind, know again, recollect

Deponent

1st Conjugation

recordor, recordārī, recordātus sum	call to mind, remember, recollect

Irregular

meminī, meminisse	remember, recollect, think of, bear in mind

• RULING

Regular	
1st Conjugation	
imperitō, imperitāre, imperitāvī, imperitātus	rule, command, govern, be supreme
imperō, imperāre, imperāvī, imperātus	rule, control, govern, exercise authority
rēgnō, rēgnāre, rēgnāvī, rēgnātum	rule, reign, be king, have royal power
3rd Conjugation	
cōnstituō, cōnstituere, cōnstituī, cōnstitūtus	regulate, arbitrate, judge, manage
regō, regere, rēxī, rēctus	rule, control, govern, sway

Deponent	
1st Conjugation	
dominor, dominārī, dominātus sum	rule, reign, govern, be supreme, domineer, be in power

Irregular	
praesum, praeesse, praefuī, praefutūrus (+ dat)	be before, be in charge of, rule

• SAVING

Regular

1st Conjugation

cōnservō, cōnservāre, cōnservāvī, cōnservātus
— keep safe, retain, guard, preserve

reservō, reservāre, reservāvī, reservātus
— save up, reserve, keep back, preserve

servō, servāre, servāvī, servātus
— save, keep unharmed, preserve, protect, make safe

3rd Conjugation

eximō, eximere, exēmī, exemptus
— free, release, let off, exempt

redimō, redimere, redēmī, redemptus
— ransom, redeem, buy back, pay for, atone for, avert

3rd io Conjugation

ēripiō, ēripere, ēripuī, ēreptus
— rescue, deliver, free, snatch away

• Saying

Regular

1st Conjugation

commemorō, commemorāre, commemorāvī, commemorātus	make mention of, relate, recount
compellō, compellāre, compellāvī, compellātus	address, reproach, summon
cōnfirmō, cōnfirmāre, cōnfirmāvī, cōnfirmātus	assert, affirm, encourage, cheer, persuade, confirm, strengthen
dēclāmō, dēclāmāre, dēclāmāvī, dēclāmātus	practice public speaking, speak with violence, declaim
dēmōnstrō, dēmōnstrāre, dēmōnstrāvī, dēmōnstrātus	mention, speak of, name, describe
dēnūntiō, dēnūntiāre, dēnūntiāvī, dēnūntiātus	announce, declare, pronounce, proclaim, denounce, order
dictitō, dictitāre, dictitāvī, dictitātus	say often, insist, plead frequently, assert
disputō, disputāre, disputāvī, disputātus	discuss, explain, treat, argue, insist
ēnūntiō, ēnūntiāre, ēnūntiāvī, ēnūntiātus	speak out, say, express, assert, reveal
explicō, explicāre, explicāvī, explicātus	explain, set forth, unfold, express, convey
memorō, memorāre, memorāvī, memorātus	speak, utter, relate, speak of, say, tell, mention
praedicō, praedicāre, praedicāvī, praedicātus	announce, declare openly, proclaim, boast, praise, commend
prōnūntiō, prōnūntiāre, prōnūntiāvī, prōnūntiātus	proclaim, announce, make publicly known, disclose, utter, decide, recite, rehearse, tell, relate, report

recitō, recitāre, recitāvī, recitātus	recite, rehearse, read out, read aloud
sonō, sonāre, sonuī, sonitus	speak, sound, utter, express, celebrate
vocō, vocāre, vocāvī, vocātus	announce, invoke, convoke, call upon, ask, invite, exhort, urge

2nd Conjugation

obtineō, obtinēre, obtinuī, obtentus	assert, maintain

3rd Conjugation

agō, agere, ēgī, āctus	speak, deliberate, prosecute, advocate, talk with, confer
dīcō, dīcere, dīxī, dictus	say, speak, utter, tell, state, assert
dīcō + causam	plead a case
disserō, dissere, disseruī, dissertus	discuss, argue, speak, discourse, examine
ēdō, ēdere, ēdidī, ēditus	relate, tell, utter, announce, declare, publish
expōnō, expōnere, exposuī, expositus	relate, explain, expose, set forth, publish, expound
mittō, mittere, mīsī, missus	send word, announce, tell, report
ostendō, ostendere, ostendī, ostentus	express, declare, say, tell, make known
praedīcō, praedīcere, praedīxī, praedictus	say before, foretell, predict, forebode, warn
trādō, trādere, trādidī, trāditus	relate, recount, narrate, hand down, pass on

3rd io Conjugation

faciō, facere, fēcī, factus	say, assert, represent, depict
+ certiorem	inform
+ verbum/epigramma/sermōnem	speak
iaciō, iacere, iēcī, iactus	mention, declare, utter

4th Conjugation

garriō, garrīre, garrīvī	chat, chatter

Deponent

1st Conjugation

adfor, adfārī, adfātus sum	speak, say to, address, accost, invoke, bid a last farewell (to the dead)
for, fārī, fātus sum	speak, say
interpretor, interpretārī, interpretātus sum	explain, expound, translate, interpret
praefor, praefārī, praefātus sum	say beforehand, say in verse beforehand, preface

2nd Conjugation

profiteor, profitērī, professus sum	declare publicly, confess openly, report

3rd Conjugation

alloquor, alloquī, allocūtus sum	speak to, address, salute, greet
loquor, loquī, locūtus sum	speak, tell, say, talk, mention, utter, speak about, talk of, murmur

Irregular

āiō	say yes, assent, assert, affirm, tell, relate (ais, ait, āiunt)
dēferō, dēferre, dētulī, dēlātus	report, announce, state
ferō, ferre, tulī, lātus	report, relate, assert, say, tell, celebrate, make known
inquam	say [after one or more words in a quote] (inquam, inquis, inquit, inquimus, inquiunt)
perferō, perferre, pertulī, perlātus	convey news, report, announce, bring home
referō, referre, retulī, relātus	repeat, relate, recount, tell, say, report

• SEEING

Regular

1st Conjugation

lūstrō, lūstrāre, lūstrāvī, lūstrātus	survey, review (troops), scan, consider, review, check, examine
prōspectō, prōspectāre, prōspectāvī, prōspectātus	look forth, look at, view, behold, gaze upon, expect, hope, look for
servō, servāre, servāvī, servātus	keep in view, watch, observe
vigilō, vigilāre, vigilāvī, vigilātus	watch, keep awake, be watchful, be vigilant

2nd Conjugation

videō, vidēre, vīdī, vīsus	see, discern, perceive, observe, look at, understand

3rd Conjugation

animadvertō, animadvertere, animadvertī, animadversus	regard, observe, see, notice, perceive, discern
cernō, cernere, crēvī, crētus	see mentally, perceive, comprehend, discern, understand
excubō, excubere, excubuī, excubitum	keep watch, be vigilant, lie out of doors, camp out
vīsō, vīsere, vīsī	look at attentively, behold, view, look after, go to see

3rd io Conjugation

adspiciō/aspiciō, adspicere, adspexī, adspectus	look at, look upon, observe, inspect, look to, regard
circumspiciō, circumspicere, circumspexī, circumspectus	see, observe, look around

cōnspiciō, cōnspicere, cōnspexī, cōnspectus	look at attentively, perceive, fix eyes on, gaze upon, observe, contemplate; (in passive: be noticed, attract attention)
īnspiciō, īnspicere, īnspexī, īnspectus	look into, inspect, contemplate, consider, examine, spy out, investigate
perspiciō, perspicere, perspexī, perspectus	perceive clearly, see through, look closely at, view, examine, inspect
respiciō, respicere, respexī, respectus	look back upon, gaze at, look for, regard, look at anxiously

Deponent

1st Conjugation

speculor, speculārī, speculātus sum	watch, spy out, observe, examine, explore

2nd Conjugation

intueor, intuērī, intuitus sum	look upon, regard, observe, look closely at

• SEEKING

Regular

3rd Conjugation

anquīrō, anquīrere, anquīsīvī, anquīsītus	seek on all sides, search after, look about
appetō, appetere, appetiī/appetīvī, appetītus	strive for, long for, seek, court, attack
conquīrō, conquīrere, conquīsiī/conquīsīvī, conquīsītus	seek for, hunt up, search out, collect
petō, petere, petiī/petīvī, petītus	seek, pursue, aim at, strive for, travel to, attack, demand, woo, solicit
quaerō, quaerere, quaesiī/quaesīvī, quaesītus	seek, look for, strive for, endeavor, strive to gain, desire
requīrō, requīrere, requīsiī/requīsīvī, requīsītus	seek again, look after, need, want, look in vain for

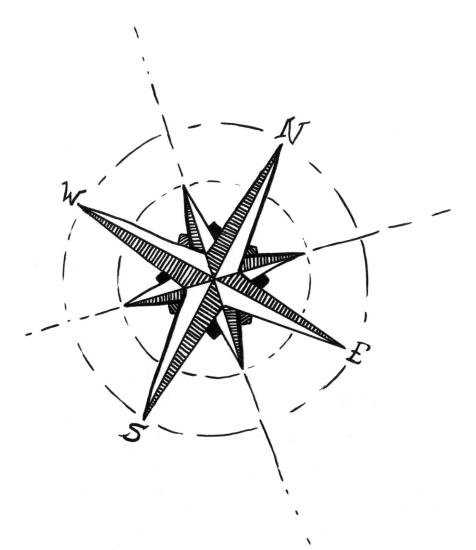

• SEIZING, TAKING

Regular

1st Conjugation

occupō, occupāre, occupāvī, occupātus	seize, take into possession, master, win
praeoccupō, praeoccupāre, praeoccupāvī, praeoccupātus	seize in advance, preoccupy
prēnsō, prēnsāre, prēnsāvī, prēnsātus	grasp, seize, catch, hold, lay hold of
pūblicō, pūblicāre, pūblicāvī, pūblicātus	confiscate, make public

2nd Conjugation

extorqueō, extorquēre, extorsī, extortus	obtain by force, extort, tear away, wrest away

3rd Conjugation

absūmō, absūmere, absūmpsī, absūmptus	take away, use up, consume
adimō, adimere, adēmī, ademptus	take away, take from, snatch away, carry off
āvellō, āvellere, āvellī/āvulsī, āvulsus	remove by force, tear away, pluck, snatch away
carpō, carpere, carpsī, carptus	pluck, pick, tear away, seize, enjoy, use
comprehendō, comprehendere, comprehendī, comprehensus	take hold of, seize, catch, grasp, detect, discover
dēprehendō, dēprehendere, dēprehendī, dēprehensus	take away, seize upon, catch, snatch, detect, discover, perceive, understand
prehendō (prendō), prehendere, prehendī, prehensus	seize, grasp, take hold of, detain, arrest

3rd io Conjugation

abripiō, abripere, abripuī, abreptus	snatch away, carry, remove, take forcibly away
arripiō, arripere, arripuī, arreptus	snatch, arrest, seize eagerly
capiō, capere, cēpī, captus	take, seize, grasp, lay hold of, catch, acquire, obtain

corripiō, corripere, corripuī, correptus	seize, snatch up, grasp, collect, take as plunder
ēripiō, ēripere, ēripuī, ēreptus	tear out, snatch away, pluck, tear, take away, rescue, deliver, free, remove
percipiō, percipere, percēpī, perceptus	take wholly, take possession of, seize, occupy, feel, observe, perceive, understand, learn
rapiō, rapere, rapuī, raptus	seize and carry off, pluck, seize, rob, plunder, carry off suddenly
surripiō, surripere, surripuī, surreptus	snatch away, take secretly, steal

Deponent

4th Conjugation

potior, potīrī, potītus sum	take possession of, become master of, occupy

• SENDING

Regular

3rd Conjugation

admittō, admittere, admīsī, admissus	send to, let go, admit, give access
āmittō, āmittere, āmīsī, āmissus	send away, dismiss, lose, let slip
arcessō, arcessere, arcessiī/arcessīvī, arcessītus	send for, invite, summon
dīmittō, dīmittere, dīmīsī, dīmissus	send out, send away, send forth, send about, dismiss, relinquish, leave, abandon
ēmitto, ēmittere, ēmīsī, ēmissus	send out, send forth, publish, set free
immittō, immittere, immīsī, immissus	send in, let in, admit, introduce, send against
mittō, mittere, mīsī, missus	send, send off, send word, announce, throw, hurl
submittō, submittere, submīsī, submissus	send as aid, send privately, let down, put down

4th Conjugation

acciō, accīre, accīvī, accītus	send for, summon, call, invite

• Shouting

Regular

1st Conjugation

acclāmō, acclāmāre, acclāmāvī, acclāmātus	shout, shout at, hail
clāmitō, clāmitāre, clāmitāvī, clāmitātus	keep yelling, yell, cry out
clāmō, clāmāre, clāmāvī, clāmātus	shout aloud, call aloud, cry out, call
exclāmō, exclāmāre, exclāmāvī, exclāmātus	exclaim, call out, cry aloud, applaud loudly
succlāmō, succlāmāre, succlāmāvī, succlāmātus	heckle, interrupt with shouts, shout after
vōciferō, vōciferāre	shout, yell

3rd Conjugation

strepō, strepere, strepuī, strepitus	shout

Deponent

1st Conjugation

vōciferor, vōciferārī, vociferātus sum	shout, yell

• SHOWING

Regular

1st Conjugation

dēmōnstrō, dēmōnstrāre, dēmōnstrāvī, dēmōnstrātus — point out, designate, show

illūstrō, illūstrāre, illūstrāvī, illūstrātus — elucidate, disclose, make clear

indicō, indicāre, indicāvī, indicātus — show, point out, inform, reveal, betray, make known

ostentō, ostentāre, ostentāvī, ostentātus — show, exhibit, present to view, show off, display, parade

praestō, praestāre, praestitī, praestitus — show, exhibit, prove, manifest, present

probō, probāre, probāvī, probātus — show, recommend, make acceptable, prove

significō, significāre, significāvī, significātus — show, point out, indicate, intimate, notify, foreshow, mean

2nd Conjugation

doceō, docēre, docuī, doctus — show, teach, make aware, prove, inform

praebeō, praebēre, praebuī, praebitus — show, exhibit, represent

3rd Conjugation

arguō, arguere, arguī, argūtus — show, prove, manifest, disclose, declare, blame, denounce

exprōmō, exprōmere, exprōmpsī, exprōmptus — show forth, exhibit, display, disclose

ostendō, ostendere, ostendī, ostentus — show, point out, exhibit, display, stretch out, hold out, manifest

3rd io Conjugation

patefaciō, patefacere, patefēcī, patefactus

disclose, bring to light, expose, make visible

Deponent

1st Conjugation

testificor, testificārī, testificātus

show, demonstrate, exhibit, bear witness, attest, give evidence

testor, testārī, testātus sum

show, prove, demonstrate, declare, assert, bear witness to

• SINGING

Regular

1st Conjugation

cantō, cantāre, cantāvī, cantātus	sing, play, recite, celebrate

3rd Conjugation

canō, canere, cecinī, cantus	sing, sound, play, make music
concinō, concinere, concinuī	sing, celebrate in song, prophesy, agree, harmonize

Deponent

1st Conjugation

meditor, meditārī, meditātus sum	sing, celebrate in song

• STOPPING

Regular

1st Conjugation

cessō, cessāre, cessāvī, cessātum — stop, delay, cease from, be idle, do nothing, pause, rest, be still

sēdō, sēdāre, sēdāvī, sēdātus — stop, stay, quiet, settle, still, calm, assuage, appease

3rd Conjugation

cōnsīdō, cōnsīdere, cōnsēdī/cōnsīdī, cōnsessum — settle, sit down, pitch a camp, stay, make a home, abate, conclude

cōnsistō, cōnsistere, cōnstitī — stop, stand still, stand, halt, take a stand, assume an attitude, settle, pause, be steadfast, endure

dēsinō, dēsinere, dēsiī/dēsīvī, dēsitus — stop, end, cease, close, make an end, desist

dēsistō, dēsistere, dēstitī — cease, desist from

resistō, resistere, restitī — stop, stay, stay behind, stand still

Deponent

1st Conjugation

commoror, commorārī, commorātus sum — linger, abide, remain, stay, dwell

moror, morārī, morātus sum — delay, stay, wait, remain, linger

• Striking

Regular

1st Conjugation

pulsō, pulsāre, pulsāvī, pulsātus	strike upon, beat, keep hitting, batter
quassō, quassare	batter, shatter, shake violently, impair
verberō, verberāre, verberāvī, verberātus	strike, beat, lash, knock, scourge, whip, flog

3rd Conjugation

afflīgō, afflīgere, afflīxī, afflīctus	strike upon, throw down, dash at, ruin, cast down, dishearten
caedō, caedere, cecīdī, caesus	strike upon, strike, beat, cut down
īcō, īcere, īcī, īctus	strike, hit, stab, sting
+ foedus	to conclude a treaty
impellō, impellere, impulī, impulsus	strike against, strike, push, inflict a blow upon, disturb, stimulate, persuade
invādō, invādere, invāsī, invāsus	assault, attack, fall upon
pellō, pellere, pepulī, pulsus	strike, beat, drive, impel, expel, affect, impress
percellō, percellere, perculī, perculsus	strike with consternation, daunt, discourage, beat down, throw down
plēctō, plēctere	beat, punish
tangō, tangere, tetigī, tāctus	strike, touch, hit, beat
tundō, tundere, tutudī, tūnsus/tūsus	beat, strike, pound, bruise

3rd io Conjugation

percutiō, percutere, percussī, percussus — strike through and through, thrust through, pierce, strike hard, beat

4th Conjugation

feriō, ferīre — strike, beat, knock, cut, hit

• Suffering, Enduring

Regular

2nd Conjugation

sustineō, sustinēre, sustinuī	bear, undergo, tolerate, hold out, bear up

3rd Conjugation

luō, luere, luī	suffer, atone for
pendō, pendere, pependī, pēnsus	suffer, pay, undergo (with poenās), weigh, be heavy

4th Conjugation

sentiō, sentīre, sēnsī, sēnsus	suffer, undergo, endure, feel the effects of

Deponent

3rd Conjugation

fungor, fungī, fūnctus sum (+ abl)	experience, suffer, perform

3rd io Conjugation

patior, patī, passus sum	suffer, endure, undergo, bear

Irregular

perferō, perferre, pertulī, perlātus	bear, suffer, submit to, put up with, endure
subeō, subīre, subiī/subīvī, subitus	undergo, subject oneself to, take upon oneself, endure, suffer
sufferō, sufferre, sustulī, sublātus	undergo, bear, endure, suffer, submit to, take up

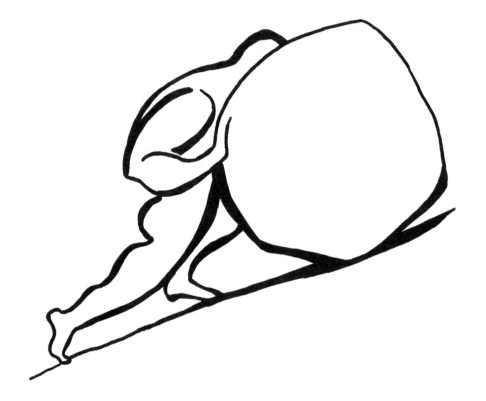

• SURROUNDING

Regular

1st Conjugation

circumdō, circumdare, circumdedī, circumdatus	surround, place around
circumstō, circumstāre, circumstetī	surround, besiege, stand around
implicō, implicāre, implicāvī/implicuī, implicātus/implicitus	encircle, envelop, entangle
vallō, vallāre, vallāvī, vallātus	surround, fortify, protect, fortify with a rampart

2nd Conjugation

obsideō, obsidēre, obsēdī, obsessus	hem in, besiege, blockade, surround, watch closely

3rd Conjugation

cingō, cingere, cīnxī, cīnctus	surround, go around, wreathe, crown
circumclūdō, circumclūdere, circumclūsī, circumclūsus	surround, shut in, enclose

4th Conjugation

amiciō, amicīre, amicuī/amīxī, amictus	surround, wrap, cover, wrap about, throw around
circumveniō, circumvenīre, circumvēnī, circumventus	surround, encircle, come around, encompass, oppress, distress, deceive
saepiō, saepīre, saepsī, saeptus	surround with a hedge, hedge in, fence in, enclose, fortify, guard

Deponent

3rd Conjugation

complector, complectī, complexus sum	surround, enclose, encircle, grasp, embrace

Irregular

circumeō, circumīre, circumiī/circumīvī, circumitus	surround, encircle, enclose, encompass, go around, travel around, visit
obeō, obīre, obiī/obīvī, obitus	surround, go over, envelop

• THINKING

Regular	

1st Conjugation

cōgitō, cōgitāre, cōgitāvī, cōgitātus	think, ponder, reflect upon, consider thoroughly
dēlīberō, dēlīberāre, dēlīberāvī, dēlīberātus	weigh well, consider, deliberate, ponder, meditate, resolve, determine
excōgitō, excōgitāre, excōgitāvī, excōgitātus	think out, devise, contrive
existimō, existimāre, existimāvī, existimātus	think, suppose, consider, judge, appreciate
iūdicō, iūdicāre, iūdicāvī, iūdicātus	form an opinion on, judge, decide, think, consider
pererrō, pererrāre, pererrāvī, pererrātus	survey, think over, look over
putō, putāre, putāvī, putātus	think, believe, suspect, imagine, consider
reputō, reputāre, reputāvī, reputātus	think over, meditate, ponder, reflect upon
volūtō, volūtāre, volūtāvī, volūtātus	think over, turn over, engross

2nd Conjugation

cēnseō, cēnsēre, cēnsuī, cēnsus	assess, estimate, think, believe, suppose, expect
habeō, habēre, habuī, habitus	have in mind, think, believe, regard

3rd Conjugation

dūcō, dūcere, dūxī, ductus	account, esteem, regard, consider
intellegō, intellegere, intellēxī, intellēctus	perceive, understand, think, discern
succurrō, succurrere, succurrī, succursum	come to mind
volvō, volvere, volvī, volūtus	think over, ponder, meditate, dwell upon, reflect on, consider

4th Conjugation

sentiō, sentīre, sēnsī, sēnsus	think, suppose, believe, perceive, discern, understand

Deponent

1st Conjugation

meditor, meditārī, meditātus sum	consider, meditate, give attention, reflect, muse
opīnor, opīnārī, opīnātus sum	think, suppose, believe, be of opinion
suspicor, suspicārī, suspicātus sum	believe, suppose, suspect, mistrust

2nd Conjugation

reor, rērī, ratus sum	think, believe, suppose, imagine

• THROWING

Regular

1st Conjugation

iactō, iactāre, iactāvī, iactātus	throw, cast, hurl, toss about, shake, flourish
praecipitō, praecipitāre, praecipitāvī, praecipitātus	hurl down, throw headlong

3rd io Conjugation

abiciō, abicere, abiēcī, abiectus	throw away, throw down, cast away, fling
dēiciō, dēicere, dēiēcī, dēiectus	throw down, hurl down, eject, dispossess
iaciō, iacere, iēcī, iactus	throw, cast, hurl, fling
prōiciō, prōicere, prōiēcī, prōiectus	throw out, throw down, throw, throw away, cast out, expel, banish, abandon

Deponent

1st Conjugation

iaculor, iaculārī, iaculātus sum	throw, hurl, cast

• Trying

Regular

1st Conjugation

temptō (tentō), temptāre, temptāvī,
    temptātus

try, attempt, experiment
upon, prove, test

Deponent

1st Conjugation

cōnor, cōnārī, cōnātus sum

try, attempt, venture, make
an effort, undertake

3rd Conjugation

adnītor/annītor, adnītī, adnīxus/annīsus
    sum

exert oneself, strive, take
pains

nītor, nītī, nīxus/nīsus sum

make an effort, strive, put
forth exertion

4th Conjugation

experior, experīrī, expertus sum

try, prove, test, attempt

mōlior, mōlīrī, molītus sum

attempt, strive, struggle,
exert oneself

Irregular

ineō, inīre, iniī/inīvī, initus

enter upon, attempt,
undertake

• TURNING

Regular

3rd Conjugation

advertō, advertere, advertī, adversus	turn to, turn towards, direct
āvertō, āvertere, āvertī, āversus	turn away, turn off, avert, remove, steal, embezzle, divert, withdraw, keep off
convertō, convertere, convertī, conversus	turn around, turn back, turn, change, alter
vertō, vertere, vertī, versus	turn, turn up, turn back, turn about, transform, change
volvō, volvere, volvī, volūtus	turn about, cause to revolve, roll, unroll, undergo

• Understanding

Regular

3rd Conjugation

adquīrō, adquīrere, adquīsīvī, adquīsītus
    understand, add to, acquire, accumulate, gain, comprehend

cōgnōscō, cōgnōscere, cōgnōvī, cōgnitus
    understand, perceive, become acquainted with, ascertain, recognize, identify

intellegō, intellegere, intellēxī, intellēctus
    understand, discern, perceive, comprehend, see into, be master of

3rd io Conjugation

percipiō, percipere, percēpī, perceptus
    understand, comprehend, perceive, learn, know, take wholly, feel

perspiciō, perspicere, perspexī, perspectus
    perceive clearly, understand, discern, note, examine

sapiō, sapere, sapiī/sapīvī
    have discernment, be wise, taste of, understand

4th Conjugation

sciō, scīre, sciī/scīvī, scītus
    understand, perceive, know, be skilled in

Deponent

1st Conjugation

interpretor, interpretārī, interpretātus sum
    understand, interpret, conclude, comprehend

• WINNING, OVERPOWERING

Regular

1st Conjugation

dēbellō, dēbellāre, dēbellāvī, dēbellātus	vanquish, subdue, finish a war
domō, domāre, domuī, domitus	overcome, conquer, subdue, vanquish, tame, break
expugnō, expugnāre, expugnāvī, expugnātus	overcome, conquer, subdue, achieve, break down, take by assault
impetrō, impctrāre, impetrāvī, impetrātus	succeed, gain one's end, bring to pass, procure
prōflīgō, prōflīgāre, prōflīgāvī, prōflīgātus	overcome, conquer, cast down utterly, overthrow, bring to an end
superō, superāre, superāvī, superātus	be victorious, overcome, subdue, conquer, have the upper hand, be superior, excel, transcend

3rd Conjugation

dēvincō, dēvincere, dēvīcī, dēvictus	conquer completely, overcome, subdue, supersede
ēvincō, ēvincere, ēvīcī, ēvictus	overcome, conquer, overwhelm, subdue
fundō, fundere, fūdī, fūsus	overthrow, overcome, vanquish, put to flight, scatter
opprimō, opprimere, oppressī, oppressus	overthrow, overwhelm, overpower, crush, subdue, press down
subigō, subigere, subēgī, subāctus	conquer, overcome, subdue, reduce, subjugate, subject, tame, put down
vincō, vincere, vīcī, victus	conquer, overcome, defeat, subdue, be victorious, prevail over, be superior, surpass, excel, exceed

• WORSHIPPING

Regular

1st Conjugation

sacrificō, sacrificāre, sacrificāvī, sacrificātus	make a sacrifice, sacrifice, offer a sacrifice
supplicō, supplicāre, supplicāvī, supplicātus	worship, supplicate, pray, kneel down, humble oneself, pray humbly, implore

3rd Conjugation

colō, colere, coluī, cultus	devote oneself to, cultivate, follow, honor, esteem
tollō, tollere, sustulī, sublātus	exalt, extol

3rd io Conjugation

faciō, facere, fēcī, factus	make offerings, make sacrifice, celebrate, esteem

Irregular

efferō, efferre, extulī, ēlātus	exalt, laud, praise, extol, raise, elevate

• WRITING

Regular

1st Conjugation

notō, notāre, notāvī, notātus	designate with a mark, mark, write

3rd Conjugation

circumscrībō, circumscrībere, circumscrīpsī, circumscrīptus	define, circumscribe
cōnscrībō, cōnscrībere, cōnscrīpsī, cōnscrīptus	write together, write in a roll, put together in writing, draw up, compose, write, write over
ēdō, ēdere, ēdidī, ēditus	put forth, publish, spread abroad, relate, tell
incīdō, incīdere, incīdī, incīsus	carve, engrave, cut upon, inscribe
inscrībō, inscrībere, inscrīpsī, inscrīptus	write upon, inscribe, brand
pangō, pangere, pepigī/pānxī/pēgī, pāctus	write, compose, make, record, betroth
perscrībō, perscrībere, perscrīpsī, perscrīptus	write in full, write at length, write out, record, register
scrībō, scrībere, scrīpsī, scrīptus	write, write out, compose, draw up, produce, say in writing, tell in a letter, tell in writing, communicate, enroll
subscrībō, subscrībere, subscrīpsī, subscrīptus	write underneath, write down, note down

3rd io Conjugation

faciō, facere, fēcī, factus	compose, write

Irregular
---

referō, referre, rettulī, relātus	note down, enter, inscribe, register, record, enroll

• Nouns

• ACCESS

1st Declension

M/F

copia, ae, f.	access, admission, opportunity
iānua, ae, f.	access, approach, entrance, door
porta, ae, f.	gate, city-gate, door, entrance, passage

4th Declension

M/F

accessus, ūs, m.	approach, access, entry, way in, attack
aditus, ūs, m.	approach, access, entrance, entry
gradus, ūs, m.	step, approach, advance, grade, stage

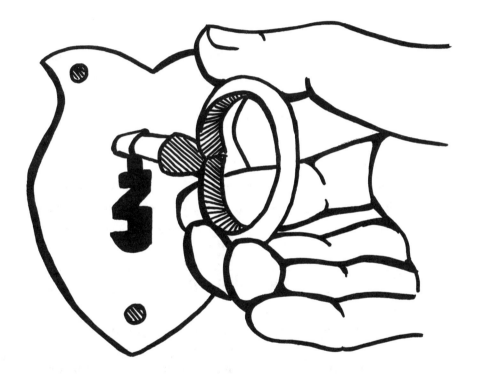

• ALLIES, FRIENDS, ALLIANCES

1st Declension

M/F

amīca, ae, f.	female friend, mistress
amīcitia, ae, f.	friendship, league, alliance, circle of friends
conlega/collega, ae, m.	colleague, associate, companion, partner in office
convīva, ae, m./f.	table companion, guest, promised guest
grātia, ae, f.	friendship, partiality, love, liking

2nd Declension

M/F

amīculus, ī, m.	little friend
amīcus, ī, m.	friend, patron, protector, companion, ally
necessārius, ī, m.	friend, client, patron, kinsman, relation
socius, ī, m.	partner, comrade, companion, associate, sharer

3rd Declension

M/F

affīnitās, affīnitātis, f.	affinity, connection; relationship by marriage
comes, comitis, m./f.	companion, associate, sharer, partner, attendant, guardian, tutor
cōmitās, cōmitātis, f.	friendliness, kindness, courtesy
cōnsuētūdō, cōnsuētūdinis, f.	companionship, familiarity, social intercourse
convīctor, ōris, m.	familiar friend, table companion
factiō, factiōnis, f.	company, association, faction
familiāritās, familiāritātis, f.	familiarity, friendship, intimate acquaintance
fautor, ōris, m.	promoter, patron, applauder, favorer

hospes, hospitis, m.	host, guest, visitor, sojourner
necessitūdō, necessitūdinis, f.	friendship, relationship, personal union, close connection, bond, intimacy
particeps, participis, m. (+ gen)	comrade, partner, fellow-soldier
satelles, satellitis, m./f.	attendant, companion, follower, accomplice, partner
societās, societātis, f.	fellowship, union, association, alliance

N

foedus, foederis, n.	alliance, compact, league, treaty

3rd Declension i-stem

M/F

sodālis, is, m./f.	associate, friend, intimate, comrade

4th Declension

M/F

comitātus, ūs, m.	escort, suite, train, retinue
convīctus, ūs, m.	intimate friendship, social intercourse, living together

• Anger

1st Declension

M/F

furia, ae, f.	fury, madness, rage; goddess of vengeance
invidia, ae, f.	hatred, grudge, jealousy, ill-will
īra, ae, f.	anger, wrath, rage, passion, ire, fury
īrācundia, ae, f.	anger, quick temper, wrath, passion, resentment

2nd Declension

M/F

stomachus, ī, m.	irritation, annoyance

N

cerebrum, ī, n.	anger, choler
odium, ī, n.	hatred, grudge, animosity, enmity

3rd Declension

M/F

furor, ōris, m.	rage, madness, fury, passion, prophetic frenzy, passionate love

3rd Declension i-stem

M/F

bīlis, is, f.	bile, anger, wrath, choler, indignation
īgnis, is, m.	rage, fury, love, passion, fire

5th Declension

M/F

rabiēs, ēī, f.	fierceness, frenzy, madness

• ARMIES

1st Declension

M/F

āla, ae, f.	wing, division of cavalry
armātūrae, ārum, f. pl.	armed men, troops
cōpiae, ārum, f. pl.	troops, army, forces, body of men
copiae pedestrēs	infantry soldiers, foot soldiers
mīlitia, ae, f.	military service, soldiery
turma, ae, f.	troop, company, squadron

2nd Declension

M/F

expedītus, ī, m.	light-armed soldier
pīlus, ī, m.	company of veteran reserves
veterānī, ōrum, m. pl.	veteran soldiers, veterans

N

auxilia, ōrum, n. pl.	auxiliary troops, military force, troops
praesidium, ī, n.	garrison, guard, troops

3rd Declension

M/F

commīlitō, commīlitōnis, m.	fellow soldier, comrade
eques, equitis, m.	horseman, rider, cavalryman, knight
legiō, legiōnis, f.	body of soldiers, legion, army
mīles, mīlitis, m./f.	soldier, foot-soldier, infantry
ōrdō, ōrdinis, m.	band, troop, company, century
pedes, peditis, m.	foot-soldier, infantry

N

āgmen, āgminis, n.	army on the march, column, troops, army

3rd Declension i-stem

M/F

cohors, cohortis, f.	auxiliary troop, allies, company, cohort
phalanx, phalangis, f.	battalion, phalanx, compact body of heavy-armed men
vires, ium, f. pl.	military forces, troops

4th Declension

M/F

dēlēctus, ūs, m.	picked men
equitātus, ūs, m.	cavalry
exercitus, ūs, m.	army, disciplined body of men
manus, ūs, f.	troops, corps, host, company, band

5th Declension

M/F

aciēs, ēī, f.	army in order of battle, front of an army

• Arms

1st Declension

M/F

armātūra, ae, f.	armor, equipment
clāva, ae, f.	club, cudgel
hasta, ae, f.	spear, lance, javelin
lōrīca, ae, f.	breastplate
parma, ae, f.	small round shield
pharetra, ae, f.	quiver
sīca, ae, f.	curved dagger
trāgula, ae, f.	hand-dart, javelin

2nd Declension

M/F

clipeus, ī, m.	round shield of metal
gladius, ī, m.	sword
malleolus, ī, m.	fire-dart, fire-brand

N

arma, ōrum, n. pl.	arms, weapons
ferramenta, ōrum, n. pl.	swords
ferrum, ī, n.	iron, sword
iaculum, ī, n.	javelin, spear, dart
pīlum, ī, n.	heavy javelin
mūrāle pīlum	mural javelin (used when fighting walls)
scūtum, ī, n.	shield
spolia, ōrum, n. pl.	arms, arms stripped from an enemy
tēlum, ī, n.	spear, javelin, missile, offensive weapon
tormentum, ī, n.	missile, instrument of torture, sling, engine for hurling
verūtum, ī, n.	dart, javelin

3rd Declension

M/F

ariēs, arietis, m.	battering ram
cuspis, cuspidis, f.	spear, lance, tip
mucrō, mucrōnis, m.	sword, sharp point, edge, sword's point

N

tegmen, tegminis, n.	shield, armor

3rd Declension i-stem

M/F

ēnsis, is, m.	two-edged sword

4th Declension

M/F

apparātus, ūs, m.	supplies, equipment, implements
arcus, ūs, m.	bow

N

verū, ūs, n.	dart, javelin

• Attack

3rd Declension

M/F

oppūgnātiō, oppūgnātiōnis, f.	attack, assault, storming, besieging
petītiō, petītiōnis, f.	attack, blow, thrust, aim

4th Declension

M/F

concursus, ūs, m.	attack, charge, assault, onset, collision
impetus, ūs, m.	attack, assault, onset, force
incursus, ūs, m.	attack, inroad, collision, impact, invasion, raid

· Authority, Power, Command

1st Declension

M/F

summa, ae, f.	highest rank, leadership, supremacy

2nd Declension

N

arbitrium, ī, n.	mastery, dominion, authority, power, will
auspicium, ī, n.	command, guidance, authority, augury, sign, omen, right, power, will
cōnsilium, ī, n.	deliberative assembly, court of justice
imperium, ī, n.	command, authority, power, supreme power, supremacy, officer, general, empire, dominion
mandātum, ī, n.	command, order, commission
praeceptum, ī, n.	command, order, rule, injunction
rēgnum, ī, n.	royal authority, kingship, royalty, supreme power, dominion, rule, authority, influence
scēptrum, ī, n.	sovereignty, royal staff, scepter, kingship

3rd Declension

M/F

auctōritās, auctōritātis, f.	power, authority, supremacy, origination, judgment, responsibility, trustworthiness, influence, reputation
dīgnitās, dīgnitātis, f.	one in high office, dignitary, greatness, majesty, dignity, authority, rank, eminence, reputation, honor
dominātiō, dominātiōnis, f.	rule, dominion, control, supremacy, tyranny
potestās, potestātis, f.	power, authority, sway, influence, political power, might

N

iūs, iūris, n.	legal right, power, authority, duty, right, justice

3rd Declension i-stem

M/F

ops, opis, f.	power, might, influence, strength
vīs, —, f. (acc vim, abl vī)	hostile strength, force, violence, power, influence

4th Declension

M/F

iūssus, ūs, m. (in abl sing only)	order, command, decree
nūtus, ūs, m.	nod, will, command
prīncipātus, ūs, m.	supremacy, leadership, chief command, first place

• BATTLES

1st Declension

M/F

īnsidiae, ārum, f. pl.	ambush, plot, snare
pūgna, ae, f.	battle, combat, engagement, contest, hand-to-hand fight

2nd Declension

N

arma, ōrum, n. pl.	war
bellum, ī, n.	war
proelium, ī, n.	battle, combat, contest, strife

3rd Declension

M/F

contentiō, contentiōnis, f.	fight, dispute, contest, struggle, effort
dīmicātiō, dīmicātiōnis, f.	fight, combat, contest, encounter, struggle

N

certāmen, certāminis, n.	decisive contest, battle, fight, struggle, rivalry, strife

3rd Declension i-stem

M/F

mārs, mārtis, m.	war, conflict, battle, engagement

5th Declension

M/F

aciēs, ēī, f.	battle, engagement

• Beginnings

2nd Declension

N

elementa, ōrum, n. pl.	beginnings, rudiments, elements
exōrdium, ī, n.	beginning, start, origin
inceptum, ī, n.	beginning, undertaking, attempt
initium, ī, n.	beginning, commencement, secret sacred rites
prīmordium, ī, n.	beginning, origin, commencement
rudīmentum, ī, n.	beginning, first attempt, trial, commencement

3rd Declension

M/F

inceptiō, inceptiōnis, f.	beginning, undertaking, inception
ingressiō, ingressiōnis, f.	beginning, walking, entering

N

caput, capitis, n.	origin, source
sēmen, sēminis, n.	origin, source, seed

3rd Declension i-stem

M/F

fōns, fontis, m.	spring, source, well, fountain-head
stirps, stirpis, f./m.	beginning, root, source, origin, foundation

4th Declension

M/F

ingressus, ūs, m.	beginning, entry, walking, inroad

• BLOOD

1st Declension

M/F

vēna, ae, f.	blood-vessel, vein, artery

3rd Declension

M/F

cruor, ōris, m.	blood, gore, stream of blood, bloodshed
sanguis, sanguinis, m.	blood, family, descent
sanguō, sanguinis, m.	blood

3rd Declension i-stem

M/F

caedēs, is, f.	shed blood, gore

5th Declension

M/F

saniēs, ēī, f.	blood, gore, foam, froth

• BOUNDARIES

1st Declension

M/F

ōra, ae, f.   boundary, limit, end, margin, border, edge, extremity

2nd Declension

M/F

terminus, ī, m.   boundary-line, boundary, limit

N

cōnfīnium, ī, n.   common boundary, limit, border, confine

initium, ī, n.   border, edge, entrance (to a country)

3rd Declension

M/F

līmes, līmitis, m.   boundary, limit, fortified boundary-line, boundary-war

regiō, regiōnis, f.   boundary, limit, visual line, line of sight, portion of country, district

3rd Declension i-stem

M/F

fīnis, is, m.   boundary, limit, border

• BUILDINGS, DWELLINGS

1st Declension

M/F

āra, ae, f.	hearth, home, altar
aula, ae, f.	palace, residence, royal court
casa, ae, f.	cottage, hut, small house, shed
īnsula, ae, f.	tenement for poor families
rēgia, ae, f.	royal palace, castle, fortress
spēlunca, ae, f.	cave, cavern, den
vīlla, ae, f.	country-house, farm, villa

2nd Declension

M/F

focus, ī, m.	hearth, home
fundus, ī, m.	farm, estate

N

aedificium, ī, n.	building, edifice, structure
amphitheātrum, ī, n.	amphitheatre
castellum, ī, n.	citadel, fortress, shelter, stronghold, castle, fort
castrum, ī, n.	castle, fort, fortress
domicilium, ī, n.	dwelling, domicile, abode, home seat
horreum, ī, n.	storehouse, barn
monumentum, ī, n.	monument, memorial
perfugium, ī, n.	shelter, asylum, refuge
praedium, ī, n.	farm, estate, manor
tēctum, ī, n.	roof, dwelling, house, shelter, abode
templum, ī, n.	shrine, temple

3rd Declension

N

culmen, culminis, n. roof, rooftop, summit of a building, height

līmen, līminis, n. house, dwelling, abode

3rd Declension i-stem

M/F

aedēs, is, f. dwelling of the gods, temple, sanctuary, room, apartment; (in plural) house, habitation (for people)

arx, arcis, f. castle, citadel, fortress, stronghold

sēdēs, is, f. seat, dwelling-place, residence, abode, temple; abode of the dead, last home, burial-place

turris, is, f. tower, high building, castle, palace, citadel

4th Declension

M/F

domus, ūs, f. house, mansion, dwelling, abode, residence

obtentus, ūs, m. cover, shelter

• CHARACTER

1st Declension

M/F

nātūra, ae, f.   character, disposition, natural disposition

2nd Declension

M/F

animus, ī, m.   character, disposition, temper, courage, spirit

N

ingenium, ī, n.   innate quality, character, temper, natural disposition, talents, genius

3rd Declension

M/F

exīstimātiō, ōnis, f.   character, honor, good name

mōrēs, um, m. pl.   character, morals, manners, conduct, behavior

virtūs, virtūtis, f.   high character, moral perfection, merit, manliness, strength, excellence

3rd Declension i-stem

M/F

indolēs, is, f.   character, genius, disposition, native quality, nature

stirps, stirpis, f./m.   inborn character, nature

4th Declension

M/F

habitus, ūs, m.   character, quality, nature

spīritus, ūs, m.   character, spirit, disposition, energy, pride, arrogance

• Charm

1st Declension

M/F

illecebra, ae, f.   attraction, charm, allurement, enticement

3rd Declension

M/F

amoenitās, amoenitātis, f.   charm, pleasantness

dulcēdo, dulcēdinis, f.   charm, delightfulness, sweetness,
                               agreeableness

lepōs, lepōris, m.   charm, grace, politeness, agreeableness,
                               pleasantness, wit, humor

suāvitās, suāvitātis, f.   sweetness, pleasantness, agreeableness

venustās, venustātis, f.   charm, grace, beauty, elegance

• CITIES, TOWNS

2nd Declension

M/F

vīcus, ī, m.	village, hamlet, row of houses, quarter, country-seat

N

mūnicipium, ī, n.	free town (whose people are Roman citizens, ruled by own laws)
oppidum, ī, n.	town, city

3rd Declension

M/F

cīvitās, cīvitātis, f.	community of citizens, state

3rd Declension i-stem

M/F

urbs, urbis, f.	city, walled town

N

moenia, ium, n. pl.	walled town, city enclosed by walls

4th Declension

N

astū, —, n., indeclinable	city

• CLEVERNESS

1st Declension

M/F

astūtia, ae, f.	slyness, cunning, astuteness
sollertia, ae, f.	shrewdness, skill
vafritia, ae, f.	cunning, ingenuity

3rd Declension

M/F

calliditās, callid? itātis, f.	shrewdness, cunning, craft, skill

4th Declension

M/F

astus, ūs, m.	cunning, cleverness, craft

• Cliffs, Rocks

2nd Declension	
M/F	
scopulus, ī, m.	rock, cliff, crag
N	
iugum, ī, n.	ridge, cliff

3rd Declension	
M/F	
lapis, lapidis, m.	stone, boundary-stone, gravestone, auctioneer's stone at slave sale

3rd Declension i-stem	
M/F	
cautēs, is, f.	rock, cliff, crag
rūpēs, is, f.	rock, cliff

• COMMANDERS

2nd Declension

M/F

praefectus, ī, m.	commander, governor, superintendent, overseer
tribūnus, ī, m.	president, commander, representative, tribune
trierarchus, ī, m.	captain of trireme, naval captain

3rd Declension

M/F

centuriō, centuriōnis, m.	commander of a century, captain, centurion
cūrātor, ōris, m.	manager, overseer, superintendent, keeper, delegate, guardian
dictātor, ōris, m.	dictator, chief, absolute ruler
ductor, ōris, m.	leader, commander, chief, general, officer, guide
dux, ducis, m./f.	leader, guide, ruler, chief
gubernātor, ōris, m.	director, ruler, governor, steersman, pilot, helmsman
imperātor, ōris, m.	general, imperator, leader, chief, commander, ruler, master
praetor, ōris, m.	leader, head, chief, commander, general
prīnceps, prīncipis, m.	first, chief, leader
prōcūrātor, ōris, m.	manager, overseer, administrator, keeper
rēgnātor, ōris, m.	governor, ruler

• CROWDS

1st Declension

M/F

caterva, ae, f.	crowd, troop, throng, band
frequentia, ae, f.	multitude, throng, crowd
silva, ae, f.	crowd, mass, abundance, supply
turba, ae, f.	disorderly crowd, throng, mob, tumult, common crowd, mass
turma, ae, f.	crowd, throng

2nd Declension

M/F

globus, ī, m.	crowd, throng, mass, gathering
populus, ī, m.	crowd, throng, multitude, host

N

vulgus, ī, n.	mass, multitude, crowd, throng

3rd Declension

M/F

celebritās, celebritātis, f.	great number, throng, crowd, multitude, festal celebration
cōntiō, cōntiōnis, f.	gathering, convocation, audience
grex, gregis, m.	crowd, throng, set, clique, flock, herd
multitūdō, multitūdinis, f.	crowd, multitude, great number, throng, common people

N

āgmen, āgminis, n.	multitude, host, throng, crowd

3rd Declension i-stem

M/F

cohors, cohortis, f.	crowd, multitude, throng, train

4th Declension

M/F

comitātus, ūs, m.   crowd, swarm, company, band, train, retinue

conventus, ūs, m.   meeting, assembly, throng

• CRUELTY

1st Declension	

M/F

| saevitia, ae, f. | rage, savageness, fierceness, brutality |

3rd Declension	

M/F

acerbitās, acerbitātis, f.	harshness, bitterness, severity
atrōcitas, atrōcitātis, f.	cruelty, brutality, fierceness, hideousness, severity
crūdēlitās, crūdēlitātis, f.	cruelty
feritās, feritātis, f.	fierceness, wildness
immānitās, immānitātis, f.	cruelty, barbarism, fierceness, savageness

• DEATH

2nd Declension

N

exitium, ī, n.	death, destruction
fātum, ī, n.	death, fate, ruin, bad fortune
lētum, ī, n.	death, annihilation

3rd Declension

M/F

nex, necis, f.	death, violent death, murder, slaughter

N

fūnus, fūneris, n.	death, violent death, murder, dead body, funeral procession, burial, funeral rites

3rd Declension i-stem

M/F

mors, mortis, f.	death, dead body
pestis, is, f.	death, disease, destruction

4th Declension

M/F

exitus, ūs, m.	death, way out, end, termination, departure
interitus, ūs, m.	death, destruction, annihilation, ruin
occāsus, ūs, m.	death, end, downfall, setting

• DEITIES

1st Declension

M/F

caelicola, ae, m./f.	god, goddess, heaven-dweller, inhabitant of heaven
dea, ae, f.	goddess
dīva, ae, f.	goddess

2nd Declension

M/F

deus, ī, m.	god, deity
dīvus, ī, m.	god, deity, divine being

3rd Declension

M/F

īndiges, īndigetis, m.	deified hero, patron deity (of a country)
Larēs, um, m. pl.	gods of places, household gods, guardians of the house

N

nūmen, numinis, n.	divine will, power of the gods, divinity, deity, god, goddess

3rd Declension i-stem

M/F

caelestēs, ium, m. pl.	the gods

N

Penātēs, ium, n. pl.	Penates, guardian gods of the family, household gods

• DESIRE

2nd Declension

N

dēsīderium, ī, n.	ardent desire, longing, wish, want, grief, regret; (with urbis: homesickness)
studium, ī, n.	eagerness, desire, study, endeavor, application, zeal, prejudice
vōtum, ī, n.	wish, desire, longing, prayer, pledge, vow

3rd Declension

M/F

ārdor, ōris, m.	heat, eagerness, zeal, animation, flame, fire
cupiditās, cupiditātis, f.	desire, passion, eagerness, longing, object of desire
cupīdō, cupīdinis, f.	longing, desire, wish, passion, eagerness, excessive desire, greed, lust, love
dēlectātiō, dēlectātiōnis, f.	delight, pleasure, delighting, amusement
libidō, libidinis, f.	desire, eagerness, pleasure, longing, caprice, sensuality, lust
voluntās, voluntātis, f.	desire, inclination, free will, disposition, good will, favor, affection
voluptās, voluptātis, f.	desire, passion, inclination, enjoyment, pleasure, delight; (in plural: public shows, games)

• DESTINY, FATE

1st Declension

M/F

fortūna, ae, f.	fate, fortune, luck, chance, good luck, Goddess of Fate, Fortune
Parca, ae, f.	Fate, Goddess of Fate

2nd Declension

M/F

colus, ī, m./f.	distaff of fate

N

auspicium, ī, n.	divine premonition, indication by augury, divination by the flight of birds, auspices
fātum, ī, n.	oracle, prediction, destiny, fate, Fate, bad fortune, ill fate, calamity, death

3rd Declension

M/F

sorōrēs, um, f. pl.	the Fates

N

ōmen, ōminis, n.	foreboding, harbinger, sign, token, omen

3rd Declension i-stem

M/F

fors, fortis, f.	chance, luck, hazard, accident, Goddess of Chance; (with fortuna: good fortune)
sors, sortis, f.	lot, fate, destiny, chance, fortune, condition, duty

4th Declension

M/F

    cāsus, ūs, m.   fate, accident, event, chance

    colus, ūs, m./f.   distaff of fate

• DESTRUCTION

1st Declension

M/F

rapīna, ae, f.	plundering, pillage, robbery
ruīna, ae, f.	destruction, disaster, overthrow, catastrophe, calamity, ruin

2nd Declension

N

excidium, ī, n.	overthrow, demolition, destruction, ruin
exitium, ī, n.	destruction, ruin, hurt, mischief, cause of ruin
lētum, ī, n.	death, annihilation, ruin

3rd Declension

M/F

dīreptiō, dīreptiōnis, f.	plundering, sack, pillaging
interniciō, interniciōnis, f.	massacre, destruction, carnage, slaughter, extermination
nex, necis, f.	slaughter, murder, violent death, death
vāstātiō, vāstātiōnis, f.	devastation, ravaging, laying waste, desolation
vāstitās, vāstitātis, f.	devastation, ruin, desolation, waste, desert

N

fūnus, fūneris, n.	destruction, ruin, fall, pest, destroyer, violent death

3rd Declension i-stem

M/F

clādēs, is, f.	destruction, injury, harm, misfortune, disaster, loss, calamity, defeat, overthrow, massacre, plague
pestis, is, f.	destruction, ruin, pest, plague, curse, death
strāgēs, is, f.	destruction, ruin, defeat, slaughter, carnage

4th Declension

M/F

occāsus, ūs, m.	destruction, ruin, end, downfall, death

5th Declension

M/F

perniciēs, ēī, f.	destruction, death, ruin, overthrow, disaster, calamity, pest, curse, bane

• Doors, Gates

1st Declension

M/F

iānua, ae, f.	door, house-door, gate, entrance
porta, ae, f.	gate, city-gate, door, inlet, entrance, passage

2nd Declension

N

claustrum, ī, n.	bolt, bar (for a door or gate); cage; prison
ōstium, ī, n.	door, mouth, entrance

3rd Declension

M/F

cardō, cardinis, m.	hinge, socket (of a door), turning point, axis

N

līmen, līminis, n.	door, entrance, threshold, barrier

3rd Declension i-stem

M/F

foris, is, f.	door, gate, opening, entrance; (in plural: double-doors, folding-door)
postis, is, m.	doorpost, post

• ENEMIES

1st Declension

M/F

inimīcitia, ae, f.   hostility, enmity; personal enemy

2nd Declension

M/F

adversārius, ī, m.   opponent, adversary, enemy

inimīcus, ī, m.   enemy, foe, personal enemy

3rd Declension i-stem

M/F

hostis, is, m/f.   enemy, public enemy, foe, stranger, foreigner

• FACES, APPEARANCES

1st Declension

M/F

figūra, ae, f.	shape, figure, form, beauty
fōrma, ae, f.	shape, appearance, looks, beauty
gena, ae, f.	cheek, eyelid, side of the face; (in plural: cheeks, eyes)

2nd Declension

N

mentum, ī, n.	chin

3rd Declension

M/F

imāgō, imāginis, f.	appearance, semblance, shadow, ancestral image, mask, statue, imitation

N

ōs, ōris, n.	mouth, face, countenance, expression, features, impudence
tempus, temporis, n.	side of forehead, temple

3rd Declension i-stem

M/F

frōns, frōntis, f.	forehead, expression, face, look, appearance

4th Declension

M/F

habitus, ūs, m.	appearance, deportment, presence, condition, attire, disposition
vultus (voltus), ūs, m.	visage, expression, face, looks, appearance

5th Declension

M/F

faciēs, ēī, f. appearance, countenance, face, look, beauty, sight, sort

speciēs, ēī, f. sight, appearance, aspect, look, view, spectacle, semblance, apparition

• FAMILY, PARENTS, ANCESTORS

1st Declension

M/F

familia, ae, f.	household, family, family servants, kindred, members of a household

2nd Declension

M/F

atavus, ī, m.	remote ancestor, forefather
cōgnātus, ī, m.	kinsman, blood-relation, relative
necessārius, ī, m.	relation, relative, kinsman, client, patron
proavus, ī, m.	forefather, ancestor
propinquī, ōrum, m. pl.	kindred, relation, relative

N

patrimōnium, ī, n.	patrimony, inheritance

3rd Declension

M/F

affīnitās, affīnitātis, f.	relationship by marriage
auctor, ōris, m.	producer, father, progenitor
cōgnātiō, cōgnātiōnis, f.	kindred, blood-relationship, connection by birth, resemblance, affinity
genitor, ōris, m.	parent, father, creator, source, origin
maiorēs, um, m. pl.	elders, ancestors
māter, mātris, f.	mother, parent, producer, source, origin
pater, patris, m.	father; (plural): ancestors, progenitors, forefathers; (with familiās or familiae): head of the household; (with patriae): father of his country
patrēs cōnscriptī	fathers of the senate
prōgenitor, ōris, m.	founder of a family, ancestor
propinquitās, propinquitātis, f.	kindred, relationship, affinity

N

genus, generis, n.	family, race, stock, origin, class, sort, species

3rd Declension i-stem

M/F

gēns, gēntis, f.	family, house, clan, breed
parēns, parentis, m./f.	parent, father, mother, procreator, ancestor; (in plural): relations, kindred

5th Declension

M/F

prōgeniēs, ēī, f.	descent, lineage, race, family

• FEAR

3rd Declension

M/F

formīdō, formīdinis, f.	fear, terror, fearfulness, awe, dread; scarecrow
pavor, ōris, m.	terror, fear, anxiety, dread, alarm, trembling, shaking
terror, ōris, m.	great fear, dread, alarm, terror, panic; (in plural): terrible news
timor, ōris, m.	fear, dread, anxiety, timidity, alarm, apprehension

4th Declension

M/F

metus, ūs, m.	fear, dread, apprehension, anxiety, terror, alarm, cause of fear

• Fields, Valleys

2nd Declension

M/F

ager, agrī, m.	land, field, farm, pasture, valley
campus, ī, m.	plain, field, open country, level place

N

arvum, ī, n.	field, cultivated land, arable field
iūgerum, ī, n.	(in plural): fields, lands
prātum, ī, n.	meadow

3rd Declension

M/F

caespes, caespitis, m.	grassy field, green field, turf

N

grāmen, grāminis, n.	grass
nemus, nemoris, n.	forest pasture, meadow with shade
tempē, —, n. pl., indeclinable	valley (between Mt. Olympus and Mt. Ossa)

3rd Declension i-stem

M/F

vallēs, is, f.	valley

• Fire

1st Declension

M/F

flamma, ae, f.   blazing fire, blaze, flame, torch, passion

2nd Declension

M/F

malleolus, ī, m.   fire-dart, fire-brand (used in war)

N

incendium, ī, n.   burning, fire, conflagration, flame; vehemence

3rd Declension

M/F

ārdor, ōris, m.   fire, flame, heat, love, intensity

fax, facis, f.   torch, firebrand; nuptial torch

3rd Declension i-stem

M/F

īgnis, is, m.   fire, brightness, splendor, rage, fury, love, passion

4th Declension

M/F

aestus, ūs, m.   fire, heat, flow, passion, raging, agitation

• Foreigner

1st Declension

M/F

advena, ae, m./f.	stranger, foreigner, immigrant
aliēnigena, ae, f.	foreigner, alien, one born in a foreign land

2nd Declension

M/F

aliēnus, ī, m.	foreigner, stranger to the family, of another house, alien
barbarus, ī, m./f.	foreigner, barbarian, stranger
peregrīnus, ī, m.	foreigner, alien

• Forests

1st Declension

M/F

silva, ae, f. forest, wood, woodland, grove, orchard

2nd Declension

M/F

lūcus, ī, m. sacred grove, consecrated wood, park
surrounding a temple

N

aesculētum, ī, n. forest of oaks

arbustum, ī, n. plantation, place where trees are planted,
vineyard with trees; (in plural): trees,
shrubs

lustrum, ī, n. wilderness, lair, den; brothel

3rd Declension

N

nemus, nemoris, n. grove, forest, wood

• GLORY, RENOWN, REPUTATION

1st Declension

M/F

fāma, ae, f.	fame, repute, reputation, renown, public opinion, glory, good repute, ill-fame, blame
glōria, ae, f.	glory, fame, renown, praise, honor, pride
grātia, ae, f.	favor, esteem, regard

2nd Declension

N

fastīgium, ī, n.	rank, dignity, elevation
praemium, ī, n.	favor, reward, prize

3rd Declension

M/F

celebritās, celebritātis, f.	fame, renown
exīstimātiō, exīstimātiōnis, f.	reputation, good name, honor, character
fulgor, ōris, m.	glory, brilliance, flash
honōs, honōris, m.	honor, repute, esteem, reputation, praise
laus, laudis, f.	glory, fame, renown, esteem, praise, commendation, merit, superiority, achievement
lūx, lūcis, f.	brilliance (of a person)
nōbilitās, nōbilitātis, f.	fame, celebrity, renown, excellence, aristocracy
rūmor, ōris, m.	fame, reputation, common opinion, rumor, report, hearsay

N

decus, decoris, n.	glory, honor, dignity, splendor, worth
nōmen, nōminis, n.	name, fame, repute, reputation, renown

• GRIEF

1st Declension

M/F

querimōnia, ae, f.	lament, lamentation, complaint

2nd Declension

N

dēsīderium, ī, n.	grief, regret, longing, wish, want, need

3rd Declension

M/F

aegritūdō, aegritūdinis, f.	grief, sickness, affliction, melancholy
dolor, ōris, m.	grief, distress, affliction, sorrow, pain, anguish, trouble, pain, ache
lāmentātiō, lāmentātiōnis, f.	wailing, weeping, lamenting, moaning, lamentation
maeror, ōris, m.	sadness, grief, sorrow, lamentation, mourning
orbitās, orbitātis, f.	bereavement, destitution, childlessness, widowhood, orphanage

4th Declension

M/F

flētus, ūs, m.	weeping, wailing, lamenting
lūctus, ūs, m.	sorrow, grief, mourning, affliction, distress, lamentation
planctus, ūs, m.	wailing, lamentation, beating of the breast
questus, ūs, m.	complaint, complaining, plaint (of a nightingale)
ululātus, ūs, m.	wailing, howling, loud lamentation, shrieking
vāgītus, ūs, m.	crying, squalling

• Hair

1st Declension

M/F

coma, ae, f.	hair, hair of the head; leaves, foliage
saeta, ae, f.	bristle, stiff hair

2nd Declension

M/F

capillus, ī, m.	hair; (in plural): hair, hairs
villus, ī, m.	hair, fleece

N

pilus, ī, n.	hair

3rd Declension i-stem

M/F

crīnis, is, m.	hair

5th Declension

M/F

caesariēs, ēī, f.	long, flowing hair

• Happiness, Delight

1st Declension

M/F

laetitia, ae, f.	joy, exultation, delight, gladness, pleasure

2nd Declension

N

commodum, ī, n.	convenience, advantage, opportunity
gaudium, ī, n.	joy, gladness, delight

3rd Declension

M/F

fēlīcitās, fēlīcitātis, f.	happiness, good fortune, luck, fertility, felicity
laetātiō, laetātiōnis, f.	joy, rejoicing, exultation
oblectātiō, oblectātiōnis, f.	delight, delighting
prōsperitās, prōsperitātis, f.	good fortune, prosperity, success

• Heavens, Air

1st Declension

M/F

aura, ae, f.	wind, breeze, heaven, upper air, air
plagae, ārum, f. pl.	ethereal regions

2nd Declension

M/F

polus, ī, m.	heavens, sky

N

astra, ōrum, n. pl.	heaven, sky
caelum, ī, n.	heavens, sky, vault of heaven, air, weather
dīvum, ī, n.	sky

3rd Declension

M/F

āēr, āeris, m.	air, atmosphere, sky; lower air; weather
aethēr, aetheris, m.	sky, upper air, firmament, Heaven, Jupiter
cālīgō, cālīginis, f.	thick air, mist, vapor, fog; gloom
Iuppiter, Iovis, m.	Jupiter; heaven, sky, air

3rd Declension i-stem

M/F

axīs, is, m.	heaven, region, clime, axis
nūbēs, is, f.	sky, cloud, gloom, mist
nūbis, is, m.	sky, cloud, gloom, mist

4th Declension

M/F

spīritus, ūs, m.	air, breeze, breath of life

• Hills, Mountains, Heights

2nd Declension

M/F

clīvus, ī, m.	hill, ascent, slope, pitch
tumulus, ī, m.	hill, mound, heap of earth, sepulchral mound

N

dorsum, ī, n.	mountain ridge, back
fastīgium, ī, n.	top, height, summit
iugum, ī, n.	height, summit, ridge, chain of mountains

3rd Declension

M/F

altitūdō, altitūdinis, f.	height, depth
vertex, verticis, m.	highest point, top, peak, summit, whirlwind

N

cacūmen, cacūminis, n.	point, peak, top, summit

3rd Declension i-stem

M/F

arx, arcis, f.	Capitoline hill
collis, is, m.	hill, high ground, elevation
mōns, mōntis, m.	mountain, range of mountains

• Injury

1st Declension

M/F

contumēlia, ae, f.	insult, abuse, affront, reproach, injury, assault, violence
iniūria, ae, f.	injustice, wrong, injury, insult, outrage, damage, harm

2nd Declension

N

damnum, ī, n.	damage, injury, hurt, harm, loss
dētrīmentum, ī, n.	detriment, loss, harm
incommodum, ī, n.	injury, inconvenience, trouble, disadvantage, detriment, misfortune, loss
maleficium, ī, n.	mischief, hurt, harm, injury, wrong, crime
malum, ī, n.	injury, hurt, harm, punishment

3rd Declension

M/F

laesiō, laesiōnis, f.	attack, provocation

N

vulnus, vulneris, n.	wound, blow, stroke

• JOURNEYS

3rd Declension

M/F

peregrīnatiō, peregrīnatiōnis, f.	traveling, travel, travel abroad
profectiō, profectiōnis, m.	departure, a setting out

N

iter, itineris, n.	journey, voyage, walk, way, passage, path, road

---

4th Declension

M/F

commeātus, ūs, m.	going to and fro, leave, absence, furlough, trip
cursus, ūs, m.	journey, voyage, way, course, passage

• LAND

1st Declension

M/F

praeda, ae, f.	property taken in war
terra, ae, f.	land, earth, ground, soil

2nd Declension

M/F

humus, ī, f.	earth, ground, soil

N

iūgerum, ī, n.	measure of land, acre
solum, ī, n.	ground, bottom, base, earth, soil, foundation

3rd Declension

M/F

caespes, caespitis, m.	turf, cut sod
tellūs, tellūris, f.	earth, land, ground

N

grāmen, grāminis, n.	grass, sod

3rd Declension i-stem

M/F

fīnēs, ium, m. pl.	land, territory, country

4th Declension

M/F

tractus, ūs, m.	tract of land, territory, district

• Law

2nd Declension

N

iūssum, ī, n.	order, bidding, command; physician's prescription

3rd Declension

M/F

lēx, lēgis, f.	law, precept, regulation, rule, motion, bill
ratiō, ratiōnis, f.	law, rule, order, reasonableness, reason

N

iūs, iūris, n.	duty, justice, that which is binding, legal right

Indeclinable

N

fās (indecl), n.	divine law, divine will, sacred duty

• LIFE

1st Declension

M/F

anima, ae, f.	life, living being, soul, person, shades, spirits
vīta, ae, f.	life, way of life, manners, existence, being, spirit

2nd Declension

M/F

sūcus, ī, m.	juice, vitality, sap

3rd Declension

M/F

aetās, aetātis, f.	lifetime, period of life, age
alacritas, alacritātis, f.	eagerness, liveliness, briskness
salūs, salūtis, f.	life, health, vigor, soundness
vigor, ōris, m.	liveliness, vigor
viriditās, viridātis, f.	freshness, greenness

N

caput, capitis, n.	life, head, leader

4th Declension

M/F

spīritus, ūs, m.	life, breath of life, spirit

• LIGHT

1st Declension

M/F

lucerna, ae, f.   midnight oil, oil lamp

2nd Declension

M/F

radius, ī, m.   beam, ray

3rd Declension

M/F

lūx, lūcis, f.   light, brightness, dawn, day, illustration,
                                         elucidation, help

N

lūmen, lūminis, n.   light, lamp, torch, daylight, day, eye,
                                         clearness, luminary

• Mind

1st Declension

M/F

   sententia, ae, f.   opinion, judgment, view

2nd Declension

M/F

   animus, ī, m.   mind, intelligence, reason, intellect, imagination, disposition, purpose, will, design; (in plural): courage, spirit

N

   ingenium, ī, n.   powers of mind, talent, intellect, character

3rd Declension i-stem

M/F

   mēns, mēntis, f.   mind, disposition, feeling, heart, soul, character, intellect, reason, judgment, thought, plan, purpose, design

4th Declension

M/F

   sensus, ūs, m.   sensation, capacity for feeling

• Money

1st Declension

M/F

impēnsa, ae, f.	disbursement, expense, expenditure
lāmina/lāmna, ae, f.	cash, money
versūra, ae, f.	loan, funding

2nd Declension

M/F

dēnārius, ī, m.	silver coin worth 10 asses

N

aerarium, ī, n.	treasury, fund
argentum, ī, n.	silver, coined silver, silver money
aurum, ī, n.	gold

3rd Declension

M/F

ās, assis, m.	unit of money
mercēs, mercēdis, f.	salary, pay wages, fee, reward, recompense, rent, income; bribe

N

aes, aeris, n.	copper, unit of coin standard, bronze
vectīgal, ālis, n.	tax, duty, revenue, rents

3rd Declension i-stem

M/F

sors, sortis, f.	wages, pay

4th Declension

M/F

reditus, ūs, m.	income, proceeds, profit, revenue

• NOISE

2nd Declension

N

convīcium, ī, n.	loud noise, cry, clamor, outcry, altercation, insult

3rd Declension

M/F

clāmor, ōris, m.	loud call, shout, cry, friendly shout, acclamation, applause; hostile call; echo, noise, sound
clangor, ōris, m.	sound, clang, noise
frāgor, ōris, m.	crash, noise, din
strīdor, ōris, m.	high-pitched sound, harsh noise, grating, squeak

N

murmur, murmuris, n.	growling, grumbling, crash, murmur, hum, roar

4th Declension

M/F

fremitus, ūs, m.	loud noise, rushing, humming, murmuring
sonitus, ūs, m.	noise, sound, din
strepitus, ūs, m.	confused noise, din, clash, murmur, rattle
ululātus, ūs, m.	howling, wailing, lamentation, shrieking

• OFFSPRING

2nd Declension

M/F

gnatus, ī, m.	son; (in plural): children
līberī, ōrum, m. pl.	children
natus, ī, m.	son; (in plural): children
posterī, ōrum, m. pl.	descendants, posterity, coming generations

3rd Declension

M/F

prōpāgō, prōpāginis, f.	offspring, descendant, children, stock, progeny, posterity

N

genus, generis, n.	child, descendant, son, offspring, posterity

3rd Declension i-stem

M/F

gēns, gēntis, f.	descendant, offspring, representative
prōlēs, is, f.	offspring, child, son, descendants
pūbēs, is, f.	youth, young men
stirps, stirpis, f./m.	offspring, descendant, progeny
subolēs, is, f.	offspring, progeny, posterity, issue, stock, race, lineage

4th Declension

M/F

fētus, ūs, m.	offspring, young, progeny
partus, ūs, m.	offspring, young

5th Declension

M/F

prōgeniēs, ēī, f.   descendants, posterity, offspring, child,
                                     progeny

• Orders, Commands

2nd Declension

N

imperātum, ī, n.	command, order
imperium, ī, n.	direction, command, order
iussum, ī, n.	order, command, ordinance, law
mandātum, ī, n.	order, command, charge, commission
praeceptum, ī, n.	command, order, rule, maxim, direction
rēscrīptum, ī, n.	imperial rescript

• Peoples

2nd Declension

M/F

populus, ī, m.   people, nation, body of citizens

3rd Declension

M/F

natiō, natiōnis, f.   people, nation, race of people

N

genus, generis, n.   race, descent, lineage, people, tribe,
                                  nation

3rd Declension i-stem

M/F

gēns, gēntis, f.   people, race, tribe

prōlēs, is, f.   race, stock, descendants

• Poetry

1st Declension

M/F

poētica, ae, f.	poetry, poetic art
rhapsōdia, ae, f.	rhapsody, book (of a poem)

2nd Declension

M/F

elegī, ōrum, m. pl.	elegiac verses, elegy
versiculus, ī, m.	little verse, line

N

cōlon, ī, n.	part (of a poem)

3rd Declension

N

carmen, carminis, n.	poem, verse, song, lyric poetry, passage from a poem
epigramma, atis, n.	epigram
poēma, atis, n.	poetry, poem, passage

3rd Declension i-stem

M/F

poēsis, is, f.	poem, poetry

4th Declension

M/F

versus, ūs, m.	a line verse, line, row

Greek Form–1st Declension

M/F

poēticē, ēs, f.	poetry, poetic art

• POVERTY

1st Declension

M/F

indigentia, ae, f.	need, poverty, indigence
inopia, ae, f.	want, lack, scarcity, famine
pēnūria, ae, f.	want, need, destitution, scarcity

3rd Declension

M/F

egestās, egestātis, f.	necessity, want, indigence
exiguitās, exiguitātis, f.	scantiness, insufficiency, scarcity
mendīcitās, mendīcitātis, f.	indigence, beggary

3rd Declension i-stem

M/F

famēs, is, f.	hunger, famine, dearth, want; violent longing, greed

---
5th Declension

M/F

pauperiēs, ēī, f.	poverty, limited means

• Prophecies, Signs, Omens

2nd Declension

N

augurium, ī, n.	omen, portent, sign, augury
auspicium, ī, n.	sign, omen, divine premonition, augury from birds, auspices
mōnstrum, ī, n.	divine omen, portent, miracle; horrible sight
portentum, ī, n.	sign, token, omen, portent; demon
prodigium, ī, n.	prophetic sign, omen, portent; monster
vitium, ī, n.	defect in the auspices, unfavorable sign, impediment

3rd Declension

M/F

sīgnificātiō, sīgnificātiōnis, f.	indication, token, sign

N

ōmen, ōminis, n.	foreboding, harbinger, sign, token, omen

3rd Declension i-stem

M/F

sors, sortis, f.	lot, oracular response, prophecy

• Prophets

1st Declension

M/F

prophēta, ae, m.	prophet

2nd Declension

M/F

chaldaeus, ī, m.	astrologer, soothsayer
dīvīnus, ī, m.	prophet

3rd Declension

M/F

augur, auguris, m./f.	seer, soothsayer, augur, diviner
haruspex, haruspicis, m.	soothsayer, diviner, inspector of entrails, prophet
prophētis, prophētidis, f.	prophet
sacerdōs, sacerdōtis, m./f.	priest, priestess

3rd Declension i-stem

M/F

vatēs, is, m.	seer, soothsayer, prophet, diviner; bard, poet, inspired singer

• Protection, Guard

1st Declension

M/F

custōdia, ae, f.	watch, guard, care, protection
pātrona, ae, f.	protectress, patroness
tūtēla, ae, f.	protection, charge, care, safeguard; keeper, ward, protector
vigiliae, ārum, f. pl.	post, guard, sentinel, watchmen

2nd Declension

M/F

praetoriānī, ōrum, m. pl.	Praetorian guards

N

praesidium, ī, n.	defense, protection, guardianship, help, escort, convoy, fortification

3rd Declension

M/F

custōs, custōdis, m./f.	guardian, preserver, keeper, overseer, protector, defender, attendant

• SEAS, BODIES OF WATER

1st Declension

M/F

spūma, ae, f.	foam, froth, spume

2nd Declension

M/F

oceanus, ī, m.	the ocean
pelagus, ī, m.	the sea
pontus, ī, m.	the sea
rīvus, ī, m.	small stream, canal, conduit

N

altum, ī, n.	the sea, the deep
fretum, ī, n.	the sea, sound, channel, gulf
prata, ōrum, n. pl. + Neptunia	the sea
stāgnum, ī, n.	lake, pool, pond, swamp
vadum, ī, n.	shallow pool, ford, sea, stream, depths

3rd Declension

M/F

gurges, gurgitis, m.	waters, sea, stream, whirlpool, gulf

N

aequor, oris, n.	sea, ocean
flūmen, flūminis, n.	running water, flood, stream, river

3rd Declension i-stem

M/F

amnis, is, m.	river
canālis, is, m.	channel, canal, conduit
fōns, fontis, m.	spring, fountain, healing waters

N

mare, maris, n.	the sea; sea water, salt water
mare nostrum	the Mediterranean
mare oceanum	the ocean

4th Declension

M/F

fluctus, ūs, m.	wave, flow, flood, tide
lacus, ūs, m.	pond, pool, lake
specus, ūs, m.	canal, channel

Greek Form – 1st Declension

M/F

Amphitrītē, ēs, f.	sea goddess, wife of Neptune; sea

• SEATS

1st Declension

M/F

lectīca, ae, f.	sedan, portable couch, sofa, lounge
lectīcula, ae, f.	small litter, sedan chair, bier
sella, ae, f.	seat, chair, stool, magistrate's seat

2nd Declension

M/F

lectulus, ī, m.	small couch, bed, funeral-bed
lectus, ī, m.	bed, couch, sofa; (with convīvālis): dining couch
torus, ī, m.	cushion, sofa, bed

N

spectaculum, ī, n.	spectator's seat
strāta, ōrum, n. pl.	bed, couch
subsellium, ī, n.	seat, low bench, judge's seat

3rd Declension

N

gestāmen, gestāminis, n.	litter, sedan
pulvīnar, āris, n.	couch of the gods, seat of honor, cushioned seat

• Ships

1st Declension

M/F

carīna, ae, f.	keel, vessel, boat, ship
cumba, ae, f.	boat, skiff, vessel; boat in which Charon transported the dead
liburna, ae, f.	fast vessel, brigantine
prōra, ae, f.	bow, prow, ship
scapha, ae, f.	light boat, ship's boat, skiff

2nd Declension

M/F

lēnunculus, ī, m.	small sailing vessel, skiff

N

nāvigium, ī, n.	vessel, ship, boat
rōstrum, ī, n.	ship's beak, curved end of ship's prow
vēlum, ī, n.	sail

3rd Declension

M/F

linter, lintris, f.	boat, skiff

3rd Declension i-stem

M/F

classis, is, f.	fleet
nāvis, is, f.	ship; (with onerāria): transport ship; (with longa): ship of war
puppis, is, f.	ship
ratis, is, f.	raft, float, boat, vessel
trabs, trabis, f.	ship, vessel
trirēmis, is, f.	trireme; vessel with three banks of oars

• SHORES

1st Declension

M/F

acta, ae, f.	seashore, seashore resort
harēna, ae, f.	sand, shore, beach, coast
ōra, ae, f.	coast, sea-coast
rīpa, ae, f.	bank, shore

3rd Declension

M/F

agger, aggeris, m.	bank (of river; with rīpae)

N

lītus, lītoris, n.	seashore, seaside, beach, strand

4th Declension

M/F

portus, ūs, m.	harbor, haven, port

• SHRINES

1st Declension

M/F

ara, ae, f.	altar

2nd Declension

N

adytum, ī, n.	holiest place, shrine, sanctuary
dēlūbrum, ī, n.	temple, shrine, sanctuary, place of cleansing
fānum, ī, n.	shrine, sanctuary, temple
sacrārium, ī, n.	sanctuary, chapel, shrine
templum, ī, n.	shrine, sanctuary, temple

3rd Declension

N

penetrāle, is, n.	inner room, inner shrine
pulvīnar, āris, n.	shrine, temple, sacred place

3rd Declension i-stem

M/F

aedēs, is, f.	temple, sanctuary, dwelling of the gods, private chapel, sanctuary (in a home)

N

altāria, ium, n. pl.	high altar, altar for sacrifice to gods

• SKILL

1st Declension

M/F

perītia, ae, f.	experience, practical knowledge, skill
scientia, ae, f.	skill, expertise, knowledge
sollertia, ae, f.	skill, shrewdness

2nd Declension

N

articifium, ī, n.	skill, talent, profession, cleverness
ingenium, ī, n.	skill, natural ability, talent

3rd Declension

M/F

calliditās, calliditātis, f.	skill, dexterity
facultās, facultātis, f.	skill, ability, capability, power, means

3rd Declension i-stem

M/F

ars, artis, f.	art, practical skill

• Slaughter

2nd Declension

N

parricidium, ī, n.	murder of a father, treason

3rd Declension

M/F

interfectiō, interfectiōnis, f.	slaughter, killing
interneciō, interneciōnis, f.	massacre
nex, necis, f.	murder, slaughter, violent death
occīdiō, occīdiōnis, f.	massacre
occīsiō, occīsiōnis, f.	killing
trucīdātiō, trucīdātiōnis, f.	slaughter, massacre

3rd Declension i-stem

M/F

caedēs, is, f.	killing, slaughter, carnage, massacre
clādēs, is, f.	destruction, carnage
strāgēs, is, f.	massacre, devastation

• Snakes

1st Declension

M/F

cerastēs, ae, m.	horned serpent
vīpera, ae, f.	viper; snake (poisonous)

2nd Declension

M/F

chelydrus, ī, m.	poisonous water snake
coluber, colubrī, m.	snake, adder
hydrus, ī, m.	snake; water snake, dragon

3rd Declension

M/F

dipsas, dipsadis, f.	poisonous snake whose bite causes thirst
dracō, dracōnis, m.	huge serpent, dragon

3rd Declension i-stem

M/F

anguis, is, m.	serpent, snake
serpēns, serpentis, m./f.	snake, serpent, crawler

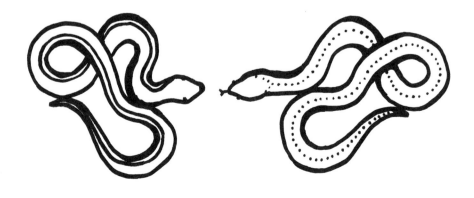

• Songs

1st Declension

M/F

cantilēna, ae, f.	old song; gossip
nēnia, ae, f.	funeral song, dirge, song of lament; cradle song, lullaby

2nd Declension

N

canticum, ī, n.	song, aria in Roman comedy, singing tone
melum/melos, ī, n.	tune, song

3rd Declension

M/F

cantiō, cantiōnis, f.	singing, spell, charm, incantation

N

carmen, carminis, n.	song, chant, incantation, charm, poem, hymn, spell

4th Declension

M/F

cantus, ūs, m.	song, singing

• Speech

1st Declension

M/F

lingua, ae, f.   utterance, speech, language, dialect

2nd Declension

N

dictum, ī, n.   assertion, remark, saying, maxim, proverb, order

verbum, ī, n.   word, saying, expression, sentence

3rd Declension

M/F

āctiō, āctiōnis, f.   delivery (of a speech by orator or actor)

contiō, contiōnis, f.   speech, pep talk

ōrātiō, ōrātiōnis, f.   speech, discourse, language, mode of speaking, oration

sermō, sermōnis, m.   talk, conversation, discourse, common talk, rumor, diction, manner of speaking

vōx, vōcis, f.   voice, sound, utterance, word, saying, speech, sentence, language

• Spoils, Wealth, Resources

1st Declension

M/F

affluentia, ae, f.	affluence, abundance, copiousness
copia, ae, f.	resources, wealth, supplies, riches, abundance
dīvitiae, ārum, f. pl.	riches, wealth, affluence
exuviae, ārum, f. pl.	spoils, booty
fortūna, ae, f.	possessions, prosperity, success
gaza, ae, f.	treasure, riches, wealth
manubiae, ārum, f. pl.	booty, prize money
pecūnia, ae, f.	riches, wealth, property
praeda, ae, f.	booty, spoil, profit, gain

2nd Declension

N

bona, ōrum, n. pl.	prosperity, property
congiārium, ī, n.	largess in money, gift, distribution
dōnātīvum, ī, n.	largess, distribution of money to the army
lucrum, lucrī, n.	gain, profit, advantage, wealth, riches, pursuit of gain, avarice
patrimōnium, ī, n.	inheritance, inheritance from a father, patrimony
praemium, ī, n.	prize, plunder, booty
spolia, ōrum, n. pl.	arms stripped from an enemy, booty, spoils

3rd Declension

M/F

possessiō, possessiōnis, f.	property, estate, possession
satietās, satietātis, f.	abundance, adequacy, fullness; disgust, loathing

3rd Declension i-stem

M/F

ops, opis, f.	means, wealth, riches, treasure, resources
vīrēs, ium, f. pl.	resources

4th Declension

M/F

census, ūs, m.	fortune, estate, wealth, riches, property
quaestus, ūs, m.	gain, profit, advantage

• STRENGTH

3rd Declension

M/F

fīrmitās, fīrmitātis, f.	strength, vigor, endurance
fortitūdō, fortitūdinis, f.	strength, force, manliness, bravery, resolution
virtūs, virtūtis, f.	strength, rigor, bravery, courage, manliness, excellence, fortitude

N

rōbur, rōboris, n.	strength, firmness, hardness, vigor, power, physical strength

3rd Declension i-stem

M/F

vīs, —, f.	strength, force, vigor, power, energy, virtue

4th Declension

M/F

impetus, ūs, m.	vigor, force, vehemence

• THOUGHT

1st Declension

M/F

sententia, ae, f.	thought, notion, opinion, way of thinking, will, desire

2nd Declension

N

cōgitāta, ōrum, n. pl.	thoughts, ideas

3rd Declension

M/F

cōgitātiō, cōgitātiōnis, f.	thinking, thought, reflection, meditation, imagination, judgment, opinion
notiō, notiōnis, f.	idea, notion
ratiō, ratiōnis, f.	reflection, reasoning, judgment, understanding

3rd Declension i-stem

M/F

mēns, mēntis, f.	thought, opinion, reason, frame of mind

4th Declension

M/F

sēnsus, ūs, m.	thought, opinion, frame of mind, judgment, idea

• Time

1st Declension

M/F

hōra, ae, f.	hour, time, time of year, season

2nd Declension

M/F

annus, ī, m.	year

N

aevum, ī, n.	eternity, never-ending time, period of life, lifetime, age, generation, period
bīduum, ī, n.	period of two days
biennium, ī, n.	period of two years
intervāllum, ī, n.	interval, intermission, respite, pause
punctum, ī, n.	(with temporis): point of time, smallest portion of time, an instant, moment
quīnquennium, ī, n.	period of five years, five years
saeculum, ī, n.	lifetime, age, generation, people of any time, spirit of the age, fashion, century
spatium, ī, n.	interval, period, portion of time
trīduum, ī, n.	three days' time, three days

3rd Declension

M/F

aetās, aetātis, f.	age, lifetime, life of man, time of life, time, flight of time, the age
posteritās, posteritātis, f.	the future, future time, posterity
tempestās, tempestātis, f.	time, season, period, point of time, portion of time
vetustās, vetustātis, f.	old age, age, long existence, long duration, the far future, posterity

N

tempus, tempŏris, n.	time, portion of time, period, season, interval, duration, appointed time, right occasion, opportunity, need, emergency, times, circumstances

---

5th Declension

M/F

diēs, ēī, m.	day, set day, appointed time, term, time, space of time, period, interval, dying-day, time to die

• UNDERWORLD

2nd Declension

M/F

Avernus, ī, m.	(Lake) Avernus; underworld
īnferī, ōrum, m. pl.	underground, inhabitants of the lower world

N

īma, ōrum, n. pl.	the underworld

3rd Declension i-stem

M/F

mānēs, ium, m. pl.	the lower world, infernal regions

• VICTORY

1st Declension

M/F

    vīctōria, ae, f.   victory, success, triumph

2nd Declension

M/F

    triumphus, ī, m.   triumph, victory, celebration of victory, triumphal procession

N

    tropaeum, ī, n.   victory, trophy, memorial of victory

4th Declension

M/F

    successus, ūs, m.   success

• WALLS

2nd Declension

M/F

mūrus, ī, m.	wall, wall of a building, city wall, protection

N

saepīmentum, ī, n.	fence, hedge
saeptum, ī, n.	fence, wall, voting booth
vāllum, ī, n.	wall, rampart, fortification

3rd Declension

M/F

mūnītiō, mūnītiōnis, f.	walls, fortification, rampart, defense
pariēs, parietis, m.	wall (of a building)

3rd Declension i-stem

M/F

saepēs, is, f.	fence, hedge, enclosure

N

moenia, ium, n. pl.	defensive walls, city walls

• WICKEDNESS

1st Declension

M/F

infāmia, ae, f.   infamy, disgrace, dishonor, ill fame, bad repute

nēquitia, ae, f.   wickedness, vileness, worthlessness, bad quality

---

2nd Declension

N

flāgitium, ī, n.   outrage, shameful act, disgrace, shame

maleficium, ī, n.   evil deed, misdeed, wickedness, crime, wrong

malum, ī, n.   evil, mischief, misfortune, calamity, wrongdoing, punishment

stuprum, ī, n.   disgrace, dishonor, violation, outrage, incest, lust

vitium, ī, n.   vice, imperfection, failing, offence, crime, violation

---

3rd Declension

M/F

improbitās, improbitātis, f.   wickedness, depravity, dishonesty

perversitās, perversitātis, f.   untowardness, perversity

turpitūdō, turpitūdinis, f.   baseness, disgrace, shamefulness, dishonor, infamy

N

dēdecus, dēdecoris, n.   disgrace, dishonor, shame, infamy; deed of shame, disgraceful act

facinus, facinoris, n.   bad deed, outrage, crime

4th Declension

M/F

lūxus, ūs, m.   debauchery, excess, indulgence

• WINDS

1st Declension

M/F

aura, ae, f.	breeze, wind, blast; exhalation
boreas, ae, m.	north wind; god of the north wind
etēsiae, ārum, f. pl.	trade-winds (NW summer winds in eastern parts of Mediterranean Sea)
procella, ae, f.	violent wind, tempest, hurricane, storm

2nd Declension

M/F

Aeolus, ī, m.	Aeolus, mythic king of the winds
Āfricus, ī, m.	the southwest wind
auster, austrī, m.	south wind
ventus, ī, m.	wind
Zephyrus, ī, m.	gentle west wind, western breeze

3rd Declension

M/F

aquilō, aquilōnis, m.	north wind

N

flāmen, flāminis, n.	breeze, wind, gale, blast, a blowing

• WORK

1st Declension

M/F

industria, ae, f.   diligence, industry, zeal, activity

opera, ae, f.   work, labor, service, exertion, effort

2nd Declension

N

ministerium, ī, n.   work, labor, employment, ministry, an office

negotium, ī, n.   labor, pains, trouble, difficulty, employment

3rd Declension

M/F

labor, labōris, m.   labor, exertion, toil, hardship, distress, fatigue, trouble, pain, work, product of labor

N

opus, operis, n.   work, labor, toil, deed, action, achievement, subject of work, artistic work, workmanship, book, composition

3rd Declension i-stem

M/F

mōlēs, is, f.   labor, trouble, difficulty

4th Declension

M/F

quaestus, ūs, m.   way of making money, business, occupation, employment, trade

• Adjectives

• AFRAID

First and Second Declension

exterritus, a, um	terrified, dismayed, panic struck
īgnāvus, a, um	cowardly, idle, without spirit
pavidus, a, um	frightened, terrified, nervous, alarmed, panicky
perterritus, a, um	frightened, terrified
timidus, a, um	fearful, afraid, cowardly, faint-hearted

• ALL, WHOLE

First and Second Declension

cūnctus, a, um	the whole, all, entire
integer, integra, integrum	entire, whole, complete, unimpaired
solidus, a, um	whole, complete, undivided, total, entire
tōtus, a, um	all, the whole, entire, total
ūniversus, a, um	whole, entire, collective, all together

Third Declension

Two-Terminations

omnis, omne	all, every

• ANGRY

First and Second Declension

īnfēnsus, a, um	furious, bitterly hostile
īnsānus, a, um	crazed, mad, insane, absurd
īrācundus, a, um	resentful, irritable, hot-tempered
īrātus, a, um	angry, irate, enraged

• BEAUTIFUL

First and Second Declension	
bellus, a, um	pretty, handsome, pleasant, nice, charming
candidus, a, um	fair, beautiful, splendid, unblemished, sincere
cōmptus, a, um	adorned, smoothed, in order
fōrmōsus, a, um	beautiful, handsome, finely formed
pulcher, pulchra, pulchrum	beautiful, handsome, fair, glorious

• BRAVE

First and Second Declension	
animōsus, a, um	courageous
bonī, ae, a	the brave (substantive)
intrepidus, a, um	intrepid, undaunted, unshaken

Third Declension	

Two-Terminations

fortis, forte	strong, powerful, mighty, vigorous, courageous, brave, manly, valiant, fearless

• Charming

First and Second Declension

amoenus, a, um	charming, delightful, pleasant
blandus, a, um	flattering, pleasant, agreeable, charming, alluring
iūcundus, a, um	pleasant, agreeable, delightful, pleasing
lepidus, a, um	charming, fine, elegant, agreeable, pleasant; effeminate
venustus, a, um	charming, pleasing, winning, beautiful, agreeable, artistic, elegant, graceful

Third Declension

Two-Terminations

dulcis, e	charming, dear, sweet, soft, agreeable, delightful, pleasant
suāvis, e	pleasant, sweet, agreeable, attractive

• CLEAR, EVIDENT

First and Second Declension

apertus, a, um	clear, plain, manifest, uncovered; frank, open, candid; outspoken, audacious
clārus, a, um	clear, manifest, plain, evident, intelligible; brilliant, famous, glorious, renowned
cōnspicuus, a, um	visible, apparent, in view, obvious
manifēstus, a, um	plain, apparent, evident, manifest; brought to light, proved by direct evidence

Third Declension

Two-Terminations

īnsīgnis, e	prominent, distinguished by a mark; notorious

• CLEVER

First and Second Declension

astūtus, a, um	shrewd, expert, crafty, cunning, sly
callidus, a, um	expert, skillful, adroit, artful, cunning, sly
doctus, a, um	expert, learned, clever, sage
ingeniōsus, a, um	clever, talented, ingenious
scītus, a, um	witty, smart, skillful
vafer, vafra, vafrum	cunning, sly
versūtus, a, um	clever, shrewd, cunning

Third Declension

One-Termination

sollers, sollertis	skilled, clever, skillful

• CRUEL

First and Second Declension

importūnus, a, um	cruel, savage, rude, harsh, unmannerly, grievous, distressing, unbridled
inhūmānus, a, um	rude, savage, barbarous, brutal, coarse, unmannerly, without culture

Third Declension

One-Termination

atrōx, atrōcis	cruel, harsh, severe, fierce, wild, savage, violent, raging, bitter

Two-Terminations

crūdēlis, e	cruel, severe, fierce, harsh, bitter, rude, unmerciful

• DEAD, PERISHABLE

First and Second Declension

adēmptus, a, um	dead
cadūcus, a, um	perishable, frail, fleeting, transitory; fallen; having no heir
moribundus, a, um	dying, at the point of death
mortuus, a, um	dead; withered, outworn

Third Declension

One-Termination

iners, inertis	dead, lifeless, sluggish, inactive

Two-Terminations

exanimis, e	lifeless; dead
mortālis, e	mortal, destined to die; temporary, transient

• Desirous, Eager

First and Second Declension

avidus, a, um	desirous, eager, greedy, covetous
cupidus, a, um	desirous, eager, wishing; greedy, covetous; amorous, loving
properus, a, um	speedy, quick, eager
studiōsus, a, um	eager, zealous, assiduous, studious, devoted to learning, learned

Third Declension

One-Termination

appetēns, appetentis	eager for, desirous of, striving after

• Destructive

First and Second Declension

damnōsus, a, um	damaging, destructive
exitiōsus, a, um	destructive, pernicious, deadly
fūnestus, a, um	destructive, pernicious, deadly, fatal
perniciōsus, a, um	destructive, ruinous, pernicious

Third Declension

One-Termination

edāx, edācis	destructive; devouring

Two-Terminations

exitiābilis, e	fatal, deadly
exitiālis, e	fatal, deadly

• Difficult

First and Second Declension	
angustus, a, um	difficult, critical, narrow, pinching
arduus, a, um	difficult, arduous, hard; high, lofty
molestus, a, um	troublesome, annoying, unmanageable; labored, affected
mōrōsus, a, um	captious, peevish, fretful, capricious, hypercritical, stubborn

Third Declension	

Two-Terminations

difficilis, e	difficult, hard, troublesome, laborious, perilous; obstinate, captious, morose, surly
praegravis, e	very wearisome, burdensome

Three-Terminations

ācer, ācris, ācre	serious, critical, severe, cutting

• Distinguished, Famous, Excellent

First and Second Declension	
amplus, a, um	distinguished, renowned, noble, illustrious
clārus, a, um	famous, brilliant, glorious, renowned
cōnspicuus, a, um	distinguished, eminent, remarkable, striking
ēgregius, a, um	distinguished, excellent, eminent, surpassing
eximius, a, um	distinguished, extraordinary, select, choice, uncommon, excellent
generōsus, a, um	noble, dignified, honorable, eminent, well-born, magnanimous, generous
inclutus, a, um	famous, renowned, illustrious, celebrated

iūstus, a, um	just, righteous, upright, perfect, complete
lautus, a, um	splendid, elegant, neat, luxurious, very grand, honorable; washed
lēctus, a, um	chosen, excellent, choice
mundus, a, um	fine, elegant, smart, clean
nōtus, a, um	known, famous, well-known
optimus, a, um	best
praecipuus, a, um	distinguished, excellent, extraordinary, special
praeclārus, a, um	distinguished, famous, excellent, admirable, honorable, splendid
probus, a, um	excellent, superior, upright, honorable
splendidus, a, um	distinguished, noble, illustrious, brilliant
summus, a, um	highest, greatest, supreme, utmost

Third Declension

One-Termination

excellēns, excellentis	distinguished, prominent, superior, surpassing, excellent, towering
praestāns, praestantis	distinguished, extraordinary, superior, excellent

Two-Terminations

gravis, e	venerable, great, eminent, influential
īnsīgnis, e	distinguished, prominent, extraordinary, remarkable, noted, eminent
nōbilis, e	famous, celebrated, noble, excellent, superior
perillūstris, e	greatly distinguished, highly honored, most notable

Three-Terminations

celeber, celebris, celebre	famous, distinguished, celebrated, honored, renowned

• DIVINE

First and Second Declension

dīus, a, um	godlike, divine, adorable
dīvīnus, a, um	divine, of a god, divinely inspired
dīvus, a, um	divine, godlike, of a deity
sacer, sacra, sacrum	holy, sacred, dedicated to a deity

Third Declension

Two-Terminations

caelestis, e	celestial, godlike, magnificent, heavenly

• EASY

First and Second Declension

expedītus, a, um	unencumbered; easy to travel
iūstus, a, um	easy, gentle, mild, moderate
remissus, a, um	mild, easy-going, relaxed

Third Declension

One-Termination

clēmēns, clēmentis	mild, gentle
indulgēns, indulgentis	lenient, indulgent

Two-Terminations

facilis, e	without difficulty, light, yielding
lēnis, e	gentle, moderate, tolerable
mollis, e	easy, gentle, soft, mild, pleasant, delicate

• Eternal

First and Second Declension	
aeternus, a, um	lasting, enduring, endless, permanent, eternal, immortal
infīnītus, a, um	infinite, endless, boundless, unlimited
perpetuus, a, um	perpetual, constant, continuous, entire, whole
sempiternus, a, um	everlasting, perpetual, eternal, imperishable

Third Declension	
Two-Terminations	
immortālis, e	undying, immortal, eternal, endless, imperishable
perennis, e	everlasting, never failing, unceasing, perpetual, perennial

• FAVORABLE

First and Second Declension

aequus, a, um	favorable, advantageous, friendly, propitious
amīcus, a, um	favorable, friendly, kind, loving, acceptable
aptus, a, um	suitable, proper, conformable
dexter, dextra, dextrum	favorable, propitious, of good omen, opportune, suitable
faustus, a, um	fortunate, favorable, auspicious, lucky, well-omened
opportūnus, a, um	fit, convenient, suitable, opportune
prōlixus, a, um	favorable, fortunate, well-disposed
prosperus, a, um	favorable, fortunate, prosperous, as desired
secundus, a, um	favorable, propitious, fortunate

Third Declension

One-Termination

fēlix, fēlīcis	fruitful, productive, favorable, auspicious, fortunate, felicitous

• FOOLISH

First and Second Declension

fatuus, a, um	foolish, silly, inane, simple, speaking by inspiration
ineptus, a, um	silly, impertinent, absurd, unfit
infacētus, a, um	dull, stupid, without wit
stultus, a, um	foolish, simple, silly, fatuous, stupid, dull

Third Declension

One-Termination

īnsipiēns, īnsipientis	foolish, unwise

• FOREIGN

First and Second Declension

alienigenus, a, um	foreign, of another land
aliēnus, a, um	foreign, alien, strange, belonging to another, not one's own
barbarus, a, um	foreign, strange, barbarous, uncivilized, of strange speech, speaking jargon, not Greek or Roman
externus, a, um	foreign, strange, of another country
īgnōtus, a, um	strange, unknown, unfamiliar, unrecognized, obscure; base, vulgar
peregrīnus, a, um	strange, foreign, exotic, alien, from foreign parts; unversed

• FORTUNATE

First and Second Declension

beātus, a, um	happy, blessed, fortunate, prosperous, opulent, rich, splendid
faustus, a, um	fortunate, favorable, auspicious, lucky
fortūnātus, a, um	lucky, happy, fortunate, prosperous, well-off, wealthy, rich

Third Declension

One-Termination

fēlix, fēlīcis	fortunate, favorable, prosperous, lucky, happy, successful

• HARSH

First and Second Declension

acerbus, a, um	harsh, bitter, sharp; grievous, severe, burdensome, distressing
sevērus, a, um	harsh, rough, rigid, severe, stern, sober, grave

Third Declension

Three-Terminations

ācer, ācris, ācre	sharp, piercing, pungent, fierce, severe

• HOLY

First and Second Declension

sacer, sacra, sacrum	holy, dedicated, consecrated, sacred; awful, venerable, detestable, horrible, infamous
sacrōsānctus, a, um	most holy, sacred, inviolable
sānctus, a, um	sacred, inviolable, holy, pure, divine, pious

• HOSTILE

First and Second Declension

adversārius, a, um	hostile, contrary, opposite, injurious
adversus, a, um	opposed, contrary, hostile, adverse
āversus, a, um	opposed, hostile, averse, alienated
contrārius, a, um	hostile, inimical, antagonistic, contrary, opposed, conflicting
īnfēnsus, a, um	hostile, inimical, enraged
īnfēstus, a, um	hostile, inimical, troublesome, dangerous, threatening, unsafe, disturbed
inimīcus, a, um	unfriendly, hostile, inimical, hurtful
insidiōsus, a, um	cunning, deceitful, dangerous, treacherous
invīsus, a, um	hostile, malicious, hateful, detested, troublesome
oppositus, a, um	standing against, hostile, opposed

• KNOWING

First and Second Declension

cōnscius, a, um	knowing, conscious, knowing in common, witnessing
doctus, a, um	learned, sage, taught, skillful, versed, trained
ērudītus, a, um	educated, learned, accomplished, instructed, informed
gnārus, a, um	knowing, skilled, expert, versed, practiced

Third Declension

One-Termination

prūdēns, prūdentis	conscious, aware, sensible, intelligent
sapiēns, sapientis	wise, knowing, sensible, sage, knowing the truth
sciēns, scientis	knowing, intelligent, understanding, skilled, versed

• LARGE

First and Second Declension

aliquantus, a, um	some, considerable, moderate, quite big
amplus, a, um	great, abundant, ample, spacious, roomy, numerous, full
īmmensus, a, um	vast, immense, boundless, measureless
magnus, a, um	large, great, big, high, tall, extensive, abundant, considerable, much
permagnus, a, um	very great, vast, immense

Third Declension

One-Termination

capāx, capācis	containing much, large, spacious, roomy, capacious
ingēns, ingentis	vast, huge, prodigious, enormous, great, strong, powerful

Two-Terminations

grandis, e	large, full, abundant, full-grown; strong, powerful; grown-up; dignified, noble
immānis, e	enormous, immense, huge, vast, monstrous

• Old, Ancient

First and Second Declension

antīquus, a, um	ancient, former, venerable, reverend, preferable
avītus, a, um	ancestral, of a grandfather, hereditary
prīscus, a, um	old, ancient, primitive, venerable, of former times
prīstinus, a, um	former, early, previous, primitive
vetulus, a, um	elderly, advanced in life, no longer young
vetustus, a, um	ancient, old, aged

Third Declension

One-Termination

senex, senis	old, aged, advanced in years
vetus, veteris	old, aged, advanced in years, ancient, former

• Other

First and Second Declension

alius, alia, aliud	other, another, different
alter, altera, alterum	the other (of two), another, one
cēterus, a, um	the other, remainder, rest
dīversus, a, um	apart, different

• POOR

First and Second Declension

indigus, a, um	in want, needing
modicus, a, um	scanty, small, moderate, modest

Third Declension

One-Termination

egēns, egentis	poor, needy, in want
indigēs, is	indigent, needy
inops, inopis	without resources, poor, destitute, indigent
pauper, pauperis	poor, of small means, scanty, not wealthy

Two-Terminations

tenuis, e	poor, inconsiderable, slight, trifling; slim, thin, delicate

• Sad

First and Second Declension

āter, ātra, ātrum	dark, gloomy, sad, dismal
fūnestus, a, um	mournful, dismal; deadly, fatal
maestus, a, um	sorrowful, dejected, despondent
misellus, a, um	wretched, poor
miser, misera, miserum	pitiable, lamentable, melancholy
tetricus, a, um	gloomy, forbidding, harsh

Third Declension

Two-Terminations

lūgubris, e	mournful, of mourning, doleful
trīstis, e	sorrowful, mournful, melancholy, downcast, dejected, disconsolate, sad

• Safe, Unharmed

First and Second Declension

immōtus, a, um	undisturbed, unmoved
intāctus, a, um	untouched, uninjured, intact
salvus, a, um	safe, unharmed, well
tūtus, a, um	safe, secure, guarded

Third Declension

One-Termination

sōspes, sōspitis	safe, sound, lucky

Two-Terminations

incolumis, e	safe, unharmed, uninjured, sound

• SAVAGE

First and Second Declension

asper, aspera, asperum	wild, savage, fierce; harsh, severe; perilous
barbarus, a, um	savage, cruel, fierce
ferus, a, um	savage, wild, rude, cruel
horridus, a, um	savage, rugged, wild, crude, rude, bristly, prickly, unkempt, with disheveled hair, unpolished
importūnus, a, um	savage, cruel, rude, harsh
indomitus, a, um	untamed, wild, unrestrained
saevus, a, um	savage, ferocious, fierce, raging, mad, cruel, harsh, severe
torvus, a, um	wild, stern, piercing, fierce, savage, staring

Third Declension

One-Termination

atrōx, atrōcis	savage, fierce, cruel, wild, harsh, severe, violent, horrible
ferōx, ferōcis	savage, headstrong, insolent, cruel, fierce

Two-Terminations

immānis, e	fierce, savage, wild, monstrous, inhuman

• SHREWD, WISE, CUNNING

First and Second Declension

acūtus, a, um	discerning, cunning, keen, acute
callidus, a, um	shrewd, expert, crafty, cunning, sly

Third Declension

One-Termination

sagāx, sagācis	shrewd, acute, keen, sagacious

Three-Terminations

ācer, ācris, ācre	acute, shrewd, sagacious, subtle

• SMALL

First and Second Declension

exiguus, a, um	small, scanty, little, inconsiderable, inadequate
minimus, a, um	very small, minute, trifling, insignificant, least
modicus, a, um	scanty, moderate, modest, small, ordinary
parvus, a, um	small, little, scanty, petty, inconsiderable
paulus, a, um	little, small
pusillus, a, um	very small, very little, insignificant, petty

Third Declension

Two-Terminations

levis, e	small, trifling, light, unimportant, slight

• STRONG

First and Second Declension

dūrus, a, um	hard, strong, solid, rough, harsh
fīrmus, a, um	strong, steadfast, stable, powerful, enduring, immovable
rōbustus, a, um	strong, hardy, firm, solid, hard, robust
validus, a, um	strong, able, powerful, robust, vigorous, sound, healthy

Third Declension

One-Termination

vehemēns, vehementis	strong, effective, active, forcible

Two-Terminations

fortis, e	strong, vigorous, powerful, mighty, steadfast, brave, manly, valiant, bold

• SWIFT

First and Second Declension

citus, a, um	quick, swift, rapid
impiger, impigra, impigrum	quick, energetic, active
rapidus, a, um	swift, hurrying, quick, impetuous, rapid
repentīnus, a, um	hasty, quick, unexpected, sudden

Third Declension

One-Termination

fugāx, fugācis	swift, fleeting, transitory

Two-Terminations

levis, e	swift, quick, light, nimble, rapid

Three-Terminations

celer, celeris, celere	swift, fleeting, quick, speedy, rash, hasty

• TIRED

First and Second Declension

aeger, aegra, aegrum	weary, exhausted, depressed, diseased
dēfessus, a, um	weary, exhausted, worn out
fatīgātus, a, um	tired, weary, worn down
fessus, a, um	tired, exhausted, worn out, weak
lassus, a, um	exhausted, tired

• UNFAVORABLE

First and Second Declension

adversus, a, um	unfavorable, contrary, opposed
alīenus, a, um	unfavorable, unseasonable, inconvenient
malus, a, um	unfavorable, bad, unsuccessful, false, unfortunate
nefāstus, a, um	unlucky, inauspicious, impious

Third Declension

One-Termination

īnfēlix, īnfēlīcis	unfortunate, ill-fated, miserable, unlucky

• VIOLENT

First and Second Declension

acerbus, a, um	violent, sharp, bitter, rough, hard
fervidus, a, um	violent, vehement, impetuous
protervus, a, um	violent, vehement, forward, shameless
tumidus, a, um	swollen with anger, incensed, enraged

Third Declension

One-Termination

atrōx, atrōcis	violent, cruel, raging, horrible, perilous
edāx, edācis	destructive, devouring
impotēns, impotentis	violent, headstrong, without self-control
vehemēns, vehementis	violent, furious, strong, forcible
violēns, violentis	violent, furious, impetuous

• WEALTHY

First and Second Declension

beātus, a, um	wealthy, opulent, rich, abundant
cōpiōsus, a, um	rich, copious, affluent, plentiful
opīmus, a, um	rich, plentiful, abundant
pecūniōsus, a, um	rich, wealthy

Third Declension

One-Termination

dīs, dītis	rich, wealthy, opulent, abounding
dīves, divitis	rich, wealthy, opulent
locuplēs, locuplētis	rich in lands, opulent, rich, wealthy

Two-Terminations

pinguis, e	fat, rich

• Wicked

First and Second Declension

dēterrimus, a, um	worst, meanest
flāgitiōsus, a, um	shameful, profligate, dissolute, disgraceful
foedus, a, um	base, shameful, vile, foul, detestable
impius, a, um	wicked, impious, shameful, irreverent, ungodly
improbus, a, um	wicked, bad, reprobate, vile, base, shameless, outrageous
impudīcus, a, um	shameless, impudent, without modesty
lascīvus, a, um	wanton, licentious
malus, a, um	wicked, criminal, depraved, malicious
nefandus, a, um	execrable, heinous, unmentionable
nefārius, a, um	abominable, nefarious, impious
perditus, a, um	corrupt, profligate, incorrigible, morally lost
scelestus, a, um	wicked, accursed, abominable, shameful
taeter, taetra, taetrum	shameful, base, abominable, horrid, disgraceful, offensive

Third Declension

One-Termination

fallāx, fallācis	deceitful, deceptive
impudēns, impudentis	shameless, impudent

Two-Terminations

infāmis, e	notorious, disgraceful, disreputable
turpis, e	shameful, disgraceful, repulsive, dishonorable

• Adverbs

• AGAIN

identidem	again and again, repeatedly
iterum	again, a second time, once more
rūrsus	again, once more, back again, in turn

• ALMOST

ferē	almost, for the most part, nearly, about, quite
fermē	nearly, almost, about, quite, closely, just
paene	nearly, almost
prope	nearly, almost, about

• ALSO

et	also, too, besides
etiam	also, likewise, and also
īnsuper	also, besides
item	also, further, moreover
praetereā	too
quoque	also

- **Because**

proptereā quod	because
quandōquidem	since, seeing that, because
quoniam	since, because

- **Before**

ante	before, previously, in front
anteā	before, earlier, formerly, previously
antehāc	before this time, before now, formerly, previously
prius	before, sooner, first, previously
priusquam	earlier than, sooner than, before
suprā	before, formerly, previously

- **But**

vērō	but, though, however, but in fact, but indeed
vērum	but, but yet, notwithstanding, still

• CERTAINLY, INDEED, SURELY

adeō	indeed, truly, so very
certē	really, surely, certainly
enimvērō	indeed, to be sure, truly
manifestō	openly, evidently
nīmīrum	certainly, surely, truly, without doubt
plānē	clearly, simply, quite, assuredly
profectō	indeed, actually, really, certainly, truly
quidem	indeed, in fact, certainly
quīn	indeed, really
quippe	indeed, certainly (used ironically)
sānē	certainly, truly, indeed, to be sure
scīlicet	certainly, obviously, to be sure
sine dubiō	without doubt, certainly
utique	certainly, assuredly, by all means
vērē	truly, really, in fact
vērō	in truth, in fact, but indeed
vērum	truly, certainly
vidēlicet	clearly, of course, plainly

• ESPECIALLY

imprīmīs	especially, first and foremost
maximē	especially, particularly
potissimum	especially, above all, chiefly
praecipuē	especially, chiefly, principally
praesertim	especially, chiefly, particularly
ūnicē	singularly, uniquely, especially

• EVERYWHERE

passim	in every direction, at random, at different places
ubīque	everywhere, in every place, anywhere
undique	everywhere, on all sides, all around, on every part

• EXCEEDINGLY, VERY, TOO

admodum	very, altogether, entirely
apprīmē	in the highest degree, exceedingly
māgnoperē	very much, greatly, exceedingly
nimis	excessively, too, exceedingly
nimium	too, too much, very much, greatly, exceedingly
valdē	very much, exceedingly, intensely, very

• Finally

aliquandō	finally, at some time, at any time, ever
dēmum	at last, precisely, only
dēnique	finally, at last, in short, briefly
postrēmō	finally, at last, last of all
tandem	at last, finally, in the end
tardissimē	finally, last of all

• FOR A (LONG) TIME

diū	all day, for a long time
dūdum	a little while ago, a short time ago, formerly
iam diu	this long time
iamdūdum	a long time ago, long before, long since
prīdem	long ago, long since, a long time ago, for a long time
tamdiū	for so long a time, so long

• FORMERLY

ante	before, previously
prius	before, first, previously
quondam	formerly, at one time

• HERE

adeō	to this, thus far, as far, so far
adhūc	to this point, to this place, thus far
hīc	here, in this place, on this occasion
hūc	to this place, to this point, so far

• IMMEDIATELY

cōnfēstim	immediately, without delay, suddenly
ex itinere	immediately, without halting, on the march
extemplō	immediately, without delay
iam	immediately, just now, presently
īlicet	immediately, instantly, at once
modo	immediately, directly, in a moment
prōtinus	immediately, at once, on the spot
statim	at once, immediately, on the spot, instantly

• JUST AS

proinde	just so, in the same manner, equally
prōut	just as, as, proportionately as
sīcut	just as, as, like, in the same way as
tamquam	just as, like as, as much
velut	just as, like, like as, even as, as if

• MEANWHILE

intereā	meanwhile, in the meantime, however
interim	meanwhile, in the meantime, however
tantisper	meanwhile, in the meantime

• NO, NOR, NOT

haud	not, not at all, by no means
immō	by no means, no indeed, on the contrary
minimē	no
minus	not at all, by no means, not
nē	no, not
nē ... quidem	not even
nec/neque	and not, nor, also not
nec ... nec/neque ... neque ...	neither ... nor
neu/nēve	and not, nor
nihil	not at all, in no respect
nōn	not, by no means, not at all
nōnne?	Not? (expecting an affirmative answer)

• NOW

iam	now, at this time, just now, at present
modo	just now, just, presently
nunc	now, at the present time, at this time
praesentī tempore	now

• ONCE

ōlim	once, formerly, of old, once upon a time
quondam	once, at one time, formerly
semel	once, a single time, ever, at some time, at any time

• Only

modo	only, merely, solely, simply
sōlum	only, merely, barely
tantum	only, only so much, alone, merely
tantummodo	only, merely

• Otherwise

aliās	at other times, at another time
alibī	otherwise, in another matter, in other respects
aliter	differently, otherwise, in another manner
secus	otherwise, differently, not so, the contrary, unfortunately
sētius	less, in a less degree, otherwise

• Perhaps

forsitan	perhaps
fortasse	perhaps, probably, possibly

• Recently

modo	lately, recently
nūper	recently, lately, just, not long ago
recenter	recently

• SINCE

deinceps	successively
quoniam	since, since then, as

• SOMETIMES

interdum	sometimes, occasionally, now and then
nōnnumquam	sometimes, a few times
tum . . . tum . . .	sometimes . . . sometimes . . .; at one time . . . at another . . .

• SUDDENLY

repente	suddenly, unexpectedly
subitō	suddenly, immediately, at once

• THEN

dehinc	then, next, from this time, hereafter
deinceps	successively, one after another
deinde	then, next, thereafter
ergō	then, therefore, consequently
hinc	next, afterwards, from this place, hence
inde	then, thereupon, after that, from that place
porrō	then, next, hereafter, afterwards
tum	then, next, afterwards
tunc	then, at that time, just then, consequently

• There

ibi	there, in that place
illīc	there, in that place
illūc	to that place
quō	there, to that place

• Therefore

ergō	therefore, consequently
ideō	therefore, for that reason
proinde	therefore, accordingly
proptereā	therefore, on that account
quam ob rem	and therefore, and for this reason
quāpropter	wherefore, on this account
quārē	therefore, and for that reason

• Thus, So

hāctenus	thus far, so far, to this extent
ita	so, thus, in this manner, in this way
sīc	thus, in this manner, so thus
tam	so, so very, so much, as much

• Until

priusquam	until, before, sooner
quoad	until, as long as, while

• WHEN, WHENEVER

quandō	(interr) At what time? When?
quotiēnscumque	however often, whenever
ubi	where, whenever
ut	when, as soon as, just as

• WHERE

is locus quō	a place where
quā	where, by what way, at which place, to what extent
quō	where, to what place
ubi	where, in what place
ubinam	(interr) Where?

• WHY

quam ob rem	(interr) Why?
quārē	(interr) Why? From what cause?
quid	(interr) Why? In view of what?
quō	(interr) Why? For what purpose?

• Conjunctions

• Also

etiam	also, and also, likewise
quoque	also, too

• Although

cum	although, when, and yet
etsī	although, though, and yet, but
quamquam	although, though, and yet, however
quamvīs	although, however much
tametsī	although, though, and yet

• And

ac	and, as well as
atque	and, as well as, together with
et	and
-que	and (enclitic, joined to and connects word with preceding word)

• BECAUSE

quia	because
quod	because

• BUT

ast	but
at	but, but on the other hand, but meanwhile
atquī	but yet, however, and yet, but somehow
autem	but, however, on the other hand
sed	but, on the contrary, but also, but in fact

• FOR

enim	for
etenim	for, for truly, since, because
nam	for, for certainly, but, seeing that
namque	for, and in fact, seeing that

• NO, NOR, NOT

nec	nor, also not, and not
neque	nor, also not, and not

• Or

an	or, or rather, whether, if
aut	or, or at least
aut . . . aut . . .	either . . . or
seu/sīve	or if, or, whether
-ve	(enclitic) or, or if you will
vel	or, or else
vel . . . vel . . .	either . . . or

• Therefore

igitur	therefore, accordingly, consequently
itaque	and so, and accordingly, therefore
quōcircā	and therefore, for which reason

• Until

dōnec	until, as long as, while

• When, Whenever

cum	when, while
quandō	when, at the time that

• Appendix: Expressions

Idioms, Phrases, Expressions

abūsiō esse	to be the improper use of a word
agere annum	to be a certain age
animum recuperāre	to regain one's senses, to wake up
causā illatā	making an excuse
conformāre + animus/mens	to educate oneself
cōnstat	it is agreed
convenit	it is fitting, proper (to)
dare operam	to give attention, take pains
dē causā	for a reason
est tantī	it is worth it
grātiam referre	to show gratitude, return a favor
grātiās agere/habēre	to give thanks
interest	it is important; it matters
istō pactō	in that way
iudicium facere	to express an opinion
libet (+ dat + infin)	it is pleasing, agreeable, desirable to . . .
licet (+ dat)	it is permitted (to)
magnā vōce	in a loud voice
magnī interest	it is of great importance
mē duce et auctore	by my influence and advice
morem gerere (+ dat)	to allow to have one's own way
necesse est (+ dat)	it is necessary
operae pretium est	it is worthwhile
oportet (+ dat)	it is right, proper, fitting

opus est (+ abl)	there is need of
placet (+ dat)	it is pleasing (to)
praestat	it is better
sē gerere	to conduct oneself, act
sē parāre	to get ready
sēmisomnus esse	to be half-asleep
tuīs verbīs	in your own words
ubinam gentium	where in the world . . .
ut opīnor	as I think
valeō (ēre, uī, iturus) ad . . .	to succeed at . . .
vēra dīcere	to speak the truth
vir optime	sir

Interjections/Commands

Age!/Agite!	Come on!
Avē!/Avēte!	Hail (or) Farewell!
Cavē!/Cavēte!	Beware! Be careful!
Ecce!	Behold! Look!
Ēheu! (Heu!)	Alas!
En!	Behold! Look!
Eu!	Well done! That's right!
Eugepae!	Hurray!
Ēvigilā!/Ēvigilāte!	Wake up!
Fer auxilium!/Ferte auxilium!	Help!
Hahahae!	Ha ha!
Heus!	Hey there!
Ignōsce mihi!	Excuse me!
Mactē!	Well done!
Mea culpa!	My fault!
Mē hercule!	By Hercules! Goodness me!
Ō mē miseram!	Oh, dear me! Poor me!
Quaesō!	Please!
Salvē!/Salvēte!	Hello!

Tacē!/Tacēte!	Be quiet!
Vae (+ dat)!	Woe on . . . !
Valē!/Vālēte!	Goodbye!
Vigilā!/Vigilāte!	Stay awake!

Interrogatives

Quam diu?	How long?
Quam longē?	How far?
Quam ob rem?	Why?
Quem ad finem?	To what end? How long?
Quid?	Why? How? What? In what respect?
Quid agis?	What/How are you doing?
Quid ergō?	What then?
Quid ita?	How is that? What do you mean?
Quidnī?	Why not?
Quid significat?	What does it mean?
Quōmodo dicitur?	How does one say . . . ?

Responses

immō	On the contrary! No!
itane?	Really?!
ita verō	Yes! Indeed!
libenter	with pleasure, gladly
minimē	No! Not at all!
nēsciōquis/quid	I don't know who; something or other
nūllō modō	in no way
nūllō pactō	in no way
quidquid	whatever . . .
quōdam modō	in a certain way
scīlicet	To be sure! Obviously! Of course! (often sarcastic)
Sī audēs	If you please . . .
vix	with difficulty

Time Expressions

brevī tempore	in a short time
cotīdiē	every day
crās	tomorrow
eō diē	on that day
herī	yesterday
hodiē	today
in posterum	for the future
māne	early in the morning
multā nocte	late at night
nocte	at night
postrīdiē	on the following day
prīdem	for a long time
prīdiē	on the previous day
sērō	late
vesperī	in the evening

• Alphabetical Index

For the purpose of the Index all verbs are here listed as infinitives.

• Index According to Part of Speech

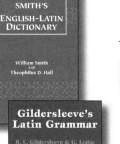

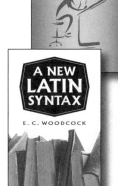

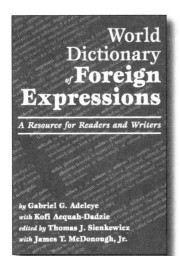

World Dictionary of Foreign Expressions

A Resource for Readers and Writers

Kofi Acquah-Dadzi and Gabriel G. Adeleye; Eds. James McDonough Jr. and Thomas J. Sienkewicz

xxviii + 411 pp. (1999)
Hardbound, ISBN 978-0-86516-422-2

The *World Dictionary of Foreign Expressions* is an excellent resource for those who encounter the foreign words and phrases that permeate spoken and written English and seek a fuller understanding of them. It contains abbreviations, single words, and phrases from a wealth of languages including Afrikaans, Arabic, Aramaic, Chinese, Dutch, French, German, Greek, Hawaiian, Hebrew, Hindi, Inuit, Italian, Japanese, Latin, Persian, Portuguese, Provençal, Russian, Sanskrit, Spanish, Turkish, and Yiddish.

Features:

- Identification of the language of origin and a polished translation for each expression
- Literal word-by-word explication of each entry
- Models for proper usage through quotations from recent scholarship or journalism
- Easy-to-follow format that is gentle on the eyes

> "... a good one-stop guide to non-English expressions that occur in English contexts ..."
> – W. Miller, Florida Atlantic University, *Choice*

> "Nothing else like this around ... The research and presentation are of the highest quality, informative, and enthusiastic."
> – Margaret Richek, Northeastern Illinois University

> "Rarely have I seen anything that is such a must-have for writers."
> – Alex Krislov, Compuserve Online Services

 WWW.BOLCHAZY.COM

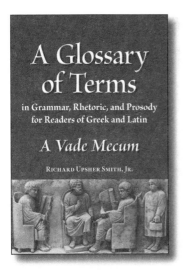

A Glossary of Terms in Grammar, Rhetoric, and Prosody for Readers of Greek and Latin

A Vade Mecum

Richard Upsher Smith Jr.

xii + 140 pp. (2011)
Paperback, ISBN 978-0-86516-759-9

From *ablaut* to *zeugma* this glossary explains terms in grammar, rhetoric, and prosody that readers of Greek and Latin commonly encounter in their first three years of study. While English grammar is the focus, the links with Greek and Latin grammar are also explained and some Greek and Latin constructions that do not occur in English are defined. Common rhetorical and prosodical terms encountered in the annotations on Greek and Latin texts are explained and illustrated with Greek and Latin quotations.

Features

- All AP* Vergil rhetorical and prosodical terms
- Quotations from Greek, Latin, and English masterpieces
- Tables of verbal aspect, types of nouns, English personal pronouns, English relative pronouns, the English verb "to be," and more

Richard Upsher Smith Jr. is a professor of Classics at the Franciscan University of Steubenville. He holds a BA in Ancient History and Biblical Studies, a MDiv from Harvard Divinity School, and a PhD in Classics from Dalhouise University. Smith served in the Angelican ministry for 20 years. He has published in the fields of Classics, Medieval Studies, and on the Reformation. Smith teaches Greek, Latin, and in the Great Books (Honors) Program.

WWW.BOLCHAZY.COM

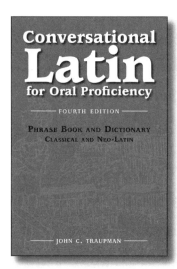

Conversational Latin for Oral Proficiency

4th Edition

John C. Traupman

432 pp. (2007)
Paperback, ISBN 978-0-86516-622-6
Hardbound, ISBN 978-0-86516-645-5
CD: (2006) ISBN 978-0-86516-635-6

Conversational Latin for Oral Proficiency is an excellent dual-language resource for exploring ancient and contemporary topics—ranging from the weather to politics—in lively dialogs with authentic Roman expression. Each chapter offers three conversations in varying degrees of difficulty supported by topical vocabulary.

The Audio Conversations CD brings the printed dialogs to life and gives students experienced guides for accurate pronunciation of Latin.

Features:

- Multi-level dialogues with authentic Roman expression
- Facing English translation
- Accent marks for all words over two syllables
- Macrons for all words
- A variety of contemporary and ancient topics, including 9 songs and The Pledge of Allegiance in Latin
- Topical vocabulary for each chapter
- A comprehensive glossary that includes the topical vocabularies for the chapters
- Appendices on "Yes and No in Latin," "Colors and Numbers," and "Sayings and Proverbs"

"John Traupman has given us an indispensable book for the active Latin classroom."

– Jeffrey Wills, University of Wisconsin

WWW.BOLCHAZY.COM